The Power of Company Culture

The Power of Company Culture

How any business can build a culture that improves productivity, performance and profits

Chris Dyer

KoganPage

First published in Great Britain and the United States in 2018 by Kogan Page Limited

2nd Floor, 45 Gee Street	c/o Martin P Hill Consulting	4737/23 Ansari Road
London	122 W 27th Street	Daryaganj
EC1V 3RS	New York, NY 10001	New Delhi 110002
United Kingdom	USA	India

ISBN   978 0 7494 8195 7
E-ISBN   978 0 7494 8196 4

British Library Cataloguing-in-Publication Data

A CIP record for this book is available from the British Library.

Library of Congress Control Number

2017001498

Typeset by Integra Software Services, Pondicherry
Print production managed by Jellyfish
Printed and bound in Great Britain by CPI Group (UK) Ltd, Croydon CR0 4YY

To all of those that I have been lucky enough to love…

CONTENTS

ABOUT THE AUTHOR

Chris Dyer is the founder and chief executive officer of PeopleG2. One of the fastest-growing companies in the US, it has appeared twice on the Inc 5000 list. Through his continued work both within his company and outside it, he has won many awards for excellence, innovation and even for rule breaking, and his company is often named as a top place to work.

Chris's passion for engagement and the success that comes about by having engaged employees is something that not only drives him but overflows to those around him. He provides real examples that help all organizations exude award-winning cultures. He does this through speeches, learning events and his globally popular live radio show and podcast, TalentTalk. Millions of people a year listen to episodes where he and his guests discuss talent, leadership, organization change and, of course, company culture. This book is heavily influenced by the conversations he has had with some of the world's top leaders and practitioners of employee engagement.

Through his work at PeopleG2, he is a recognized authority on the human capital intelligence process, and best practices for background checks. He understands the complex challenges inherent to talent management decisions, and shares these in his keynote speeches on culture, employee engagement and virtual workforces. Chris also consults for companies in order to improve their cultures, so that he can learn and grow every day. When he is not working on company culture, you can find him recording and releasing records with his band, going on adventures with friends, climbing tall mountains with his youngest son, Vladimir, or travelling with his wife, Jody. He also has two older children, Luba and Dmitri.

Finally, you can always count on Chris having a few side projects in order to stay sharp and fresh. He is a certified Scrum Master, runs two book clubs for Senior Level and HR professionals in Southern California, and often is asked to judge entrepreneurial showcases and contests.

ACKNOWLEDGEMENTS

When I eagerly agreed to write this book, no one told me how hard it would be, especially on those around me. The countless hours of writing meant time away from my family and friends, as well as leaning on my employees, mentors, friends and associates. Without all of you, not only would my book have never been finished, but my life would be empty and unfilled. To all of you, thank you.

Somewhere deep in the manual for how to be a husband must be the advice of naming your wife first and foremost in any book, speech or other public offering. My wife Jody Dyer has certainly earned that distinction, with all her love, support and the swift kicks to the pants when I wanted to be lazy and skip writing. Her edits, critiques and encouraging words can be found in every chapter. Thank you, Jody! To my son Vladimir, thank you for accepting less time with me during this process, and for being my generational sounding board. To my work staff, you all deserve the biggest green flag of all time. There are too many of you to name and account for your help properly, but please know how much I appreciate you. A few people at work do need to be named: a big thank you goes to Mike Bankhead for helping me with the book logistics, marketing and permissions. Also to my brother Bryan Dyer for picking up the slack, thank you, especially in the last month of this process as my focus waned. My dear friends Mark Gabbe, Holly Frye, Tina Kalogeropoulos, Ken Eiden and mother-in-law Anita Caruso deserve thanks for checking in on me, and providing encouragement when I was stressed out.

There were also people who helped me immensely with the book. Nancy Oso deserves a giant thank you for all her help in editing the book. The publisher of this book, Kogan Page, has been a tremendous help in getting me here, and I appreciate the confidence they have always shown in me. Sophia Levine is a saint with her enthusiasm, fantastic notes and help. Additionally, Lucy Carter and the rest of the Kogan Page team did a tremendous job behind the scenes, making it look easy. I also owe a debt of gratitude to my friends and colleagues who helped me read over the book in the final hours to ensure no errors were left. Thank you to Tenny Poole, Mike DeSon, Tania Gasca, Tami Eiden, Denise Griffiths and Brian Arandez.

Lastly, thank you to everyone who has ever believed in me. Life is often about jumping on a moving a train and being excited about where it might take you. Some of the best mentors have driven those trains for me, and it has made all the difference. Thank you so much to Kim Shepherd, Dave Berkus, Mark Goulston, Danny Kalman, Bob Kelley, Mimi Grant and everyone at ABL. To anyone I have missed or overlooked, please forgive me. It was not intentional.

FOREWORD
by Mark Goulston

Author of *Just Listen*: *Discover the secret to getting through to absolutely anyone*

Culture is the bedrock of business success. As Chris Dyer says, it 'is the combination of the easily seen ideals like vision statements and values, combined with the harder-to-see norms, behaviours, languages, beliefs and systems'. In *The Power of Company Culture*, Chris shows business leaders and HR professionals how to spot the symptoms of a culture in crisis and address issues before they impact both the business and employees. However, more than that, in this book Chris Dyer does a deep dive into the Seven Pillars of Cultural Success. These are:

- transparency
- positivity
- measurement
- acknowledgment
- uniqueness
- listening
- mistakes

In so doing he has laid out the foundation for a company culture where people feel safe to trust. The first stage of Erik Erikson's psychosocial model of development is 'trust vs mistrust'. By that he meant that if you step into the world trusting or step into the world mistrusting, your life will be dramatically different. The same can be said about stepping into a company whose culture you trust versus one you mistrust. If you don't agree with that, imagine how safe your people or even you would feel in trusting your company if:

- instead of *transparency*, there was obfuscation, and even intentional deceit
- instead of *positivity*, there was negativity, criticism and rampant fear of speaking up or out

- instead of *measurement*, there was performance assessment based on subjective interpretation

- instead of *acknowledgment*, there was a blatant absence of letting people know of their good work

- instead of *uniqueness*, there was explicit or implicit punishment for veering away from conformity

- instead of *listening*, there was talking over, at or down to people

- instead of *mistakes* being allowed for or invited, there was a deep fear of letting anyone know when you've made one

I think you get the point. This makes Chris's book an indispensable guide for everyone needing to build a better culture, and particularly trust, in their workplace.

In my line of work, I am especially sensitive to how people communicate with others. To that end, the Gold Standard is when people listen *receptively* (as in you really feel they get where you're coming from and where you want to go) and then talk *with* you so that you can easily hear, read and absorb what they're saying. With this book you feel Chris has listened receptively to you and heard your needs and then you will feel that is talking with you in a way that is easy to absorb. It's also rare to read stories and case histories that are written in a way where you easily grasp the lessons they are teaching but Chris's book is packed full of these insights and lessons.

What has always impressed me about Chris – something I am so glad comes through in this book – is his voice and tone. He is someone who always wants to help people bring out their best and be the best that they can be. This is true in person and now through this book.

Introduction

My story

One Monday following a holiday weekend, I went to work, paralysed, teetering between action and nothingness. As the CEO and founder of PeopleG2, a US company that provides employment screening and background checks to firms around the globe, decision making was embedded in my job description. But on this Monday, I found it nearly impossible to make a move – any move – let alone a productive one. My company was struggling with a major economic recession, better known in the United States as the 'heart attack of 2009'. Had all been right within PeopleG2, we might have muddled through the tough times, emerging weaker but not beaten. Or we might have succumbed to the jolt and gone under, as so many other businesses did. But something *was* amiss, and I owe my company's recovery and today's solid success to that potentially fatal flaw. It forced me into action.

You cannot fix what's broken if you don't know something is broken – or if you are aware that something is faulty but cannot identify what it is. Fortunately for the sake of such discovery, I had spent the festive weekend in a state of deep foreboding, trying to put my finger on those what-ifs. This did not sit well with my friends and family, who had gathered with me to commemorate Independence Day that Saturday. The Fourth of July serves as an excuse to socialize, barbecue, let off fireworks and celebrate our country's move in 1776 from British colony to independent nation. Amid the distraction of hot dogs, potato salad, beer and firecrackers, my mind was preoccupied. I vaguely remember friends whispering about me, in passing: 'Is Chris OK?' 'What's going on with him?' 'Give that poor guy another beer.' But, even if they had asked me what was wrong, I couldn't have told them.

As Monday 6 July 2009 rolled around, I carried this sense of unnamed dread with me to the office. It felt as though an overpowering fog surrounded my brain. Ever since I was a child, when life grows chaotic or too intense, I sense a fog rolling in, dulling my senses and rendering me incapable of making decisions – from which shoes to wear on up to the important stuff.

If you have ever been to San Francisco or London on a summer day, you know what I am talking about, weather-wise. One moment you are walking around in shorts and a T-shirt, feeling like you didn't put on enough sunscreen. The next moment, the fog rolls in and covers the city with a grey blanket of cool mist. Suddenly, you are freezing, you cannot see anything and you wish you had brought a jacket.

On that 'foggy' 6 July, I faced a morning full of appointments and a backlog of e-mails that needed replies. Somehow, I stumbled through them, and finally got a moment to think. Sitting in my trusty old black office chair, mental exhaustion washed over me. As it subsided, I was left with a disheartening epiphany. This unwelcome insight foreshadowed what I needed to do, and it wouldn't be easy. A grim realization took hold, that after more than 72 hours of thinking on the subject, my only conclusion was that I had a lot more thinking to do. But, somewhere in the back of my mind, I felt that the truth lay within, not without. This wasn't the best news. But it gave me hope. Maybe there was a final answer. Maybe I would find it.

That was the turning point.

I called my wife, Jody, who was on summer break from teaching, and told her that something had come up at the office and that I would be staying late. In fact, I told her that I would not be coming home until I had my problem sorted out – probably not in time for dinner, and I might even sleep there, if necessary. To her credit, there was no argument. She knew what I was up against.

The economic downturn had hit businesses hard, and hiring freezes were common. A reduction in human resources (HR) activity directly affected the volume of work and income at PeopleG2. Staff morale sank along with profits. The pressure of clients not ordering, not paying bills and, even worse, shutting their doors, had a chilling effect on my personnel. Even though I put on an obviously false brave face, everyone knew what was happening. In hindsight, I think they would have preferred that I freaked out, instead of half-heartedly pretending everything would be okay. If the uncertainty and pressure were intense for them, for me the situation was practically unbearable. Yet I couldn't escape it.

At that point in my company's history, we were all at one location. As it happened, my office stood along a narrow hallway that everyone had to pass to reach the restroom. The size of the space was ideal, but foot traffic in front of my floor-to-ceiling glass walls was not. What I needed was some privacy. Clearly, though, I wasn't going to get it, and I couldn't let that stop me. If PeopleG2 was to survive this heart attack, an objective examination – and, possibly, surgery – was in order. What was the sickness plaguing the company, and where did it lie? I closed the door and grabbed some dry-erase markers. Then I began to write on my glass walls.

The sharp smell of dry-erase ink filled the air and cut through my mental fog. I picked up momentum. I wrote with purpose, furiously, and my uncharacteristic fervour no doubt drew some attention and raised eyebrows. Thinking back, some of the things I wrote on that glass were not HR-friendly. Circumstances demanded brutal honesty and, left to my own devices, I brought it to the surface. I had to start somewhere. So I asked myself: at base, what was wrong with our company? And what was right?

I plotted a table listing every major aspect of company operations, with two empty columns to fill. What were the pluses? What were the minuses? The minus list was by far the longer. It included all the real and potential threats to a service-oriented business and every roadblock, from the obvious to the worst-possible scenarios. We already faced a landslide. Revenue was down, sales channels had dried up and no one was buying. In fact, clients were declaring bankruptcy or giving up, leaving in their wake unpaid invoices and a cash-flow crisis that triggered further instability.

Great. After hours of ruminating and scribbling, I knew what the result was, but not the underlying problem or any possible solution.

At last the click of staplers, the *ding* of the microwave and the voices of our verifications team diminished. My staff left for the day and I was finally in the office alone. After a weekend of fireworks and a day of frenzied thinking, the silence thrust me into deeper self-reflection. Yes, the economy was in the toilet. But that was an outside force over which I had no control. While lots of businesses were folding, many that faced even greater odds were not. Why? The answer had to come from within those organizations. What was so different about how their people handled uncertainty and strife?

I read over my lists – pluses and minuses that every company experienced – and, gradually, I found the answer. In the face of change, my staff were fighting, failing and frightened. We were not holding together; it was every man/woman for himself or herself. Our company culture was broken. Worst of all: *it was my fault.*

How did it happen? Why didn't I see it coming?

Hindsight as insight

All I could do was look back. About a month earlier, I'd had a small inkling that we might have a cultural problem. There were a few signs. The most obvious one came during a sales seminar. Knowing that we needed to expand our sales efforts and rethink our approach, specifically targets and messaging, I had my accounts team, as well as managers and support staff, come in for a special training. We needed sales more than anything else; therefore, I had decided, everyone in my organization was going to sell. This might seem a bit dramatic, but at the time it felt like the key to survival. With everyone charged to make calls, ask for referrals and think about growth, the tone was set.

So I stood in front of my staff, reading from a PowerPoint presentation and lecturing them about the importance of implementing a new sales strategy. For a few tedious hours, we did a full in-depth review of our service features and benefits. This was supposed to prepare us to win new clients, increase sales and come out ahead in a very competitive and shrinking market. Unfortunately, we failed – miserably – to identify one crucial element of what we had to offer: *us*. Our combined value. The things that, due to our expertise and way of doing business, only we could provide.

Instead of homing in on our unique selling points, I noted things like: 'We have the best customer service', 'We have the best software', 'We have...' You get the picture. It was a laundry list of boring items that any of our competitors could claim to have.

We set out to make our calls the next morning. Listening to my staff regurgitate the same trite features that every other company was touting turned out to be ridiculously depressing. This useless tactic returned to haunt me as I sat there on that dismal Monday, alone in my glasshouse of an office, determined to change course. I realized it was time for me to go deeper, beyond one size fits all. To learn what was right for *my* company in the current economic climate, I would have to both understand the strengths and weaknesses of our corporate structure and how these compared in the marketplace. I needed to look at other companies, the best ones, and discover what made *them* special and successful. Those things might, I thought, be a reflection of what made a company's employees happy to work there and happy to stay there.

This was my second epiphany of the day, but it didn't get me much closer than my original realization that PeopleG2 was suffering from a severe, innate imbalance. Again I was left with questions, and again I knew I had hard work before me in order to reach a diagnosis. Forget the economy. It was time to seek truths about myself and those with whom I worked. How could my employees best perform their jobs – not just to my mind, but to theirs, and within the full scope of their abilities? What did our clients care about? What made PeopleG2 – and the people in it – special?

My questions stoked a passion for the subject. The answers I found turned that passion into an obsession that I didn't bother to keep to myself. I talked about culture so much to anyone who would listen that my colleagues thought I should pass along the information I had collected. A common response to my enthusiasm was, 'Chris, you never shut up about all the things you read and learn at conferences. Wouldn't it be great if more people understood these things, other than just your employees?' So after expounding on the subject on a business radio show, I couldn't really say no when approached by the station producer with an offer to host my own show. He had noticed not just my zeal, but the value that listeners could gain by focusing on workplace culture.

This occurred after I had righted my corporate ship, which allowed me to bring a dual perspective to the show, TalentTalk. I could easily discuss both sides of the culture coin. Each week since 2013, I have interviewed two thought leaders who are well-respected innovators in their field, to talk about the nuances of business talent. The show is broadcast on several syndicated internet radio stations, and released as a podcast on iTunes and iHeart Radio. In asking how we can attract good talent, make the right choices to fit skills to positions, and maintain a dynamic working relationship, I am really asking how people drive business success. Some of the best ideas and conversations I have had around culture have occurred live, on air.

The gems from those interviews became the basis for many of the stories and examples in this book, as the guests gave such compelling responses to my questions. It is here that I finally defined what company culture really is from one company to the next. Company culture is the combination of the easily seen ideals such as vision statements and values, combined with the harder-to-see norms, behaviours, languages, beliefs and systems. Keep your ears open, and you will soon form your own research pool on the topic.

Spreading the word

Once I tuned into the power of company culture, I saw the news spreading from every direction – promoted by the business leaders I interviewed and the innovative companies profiled in industry magazines. With the topic on my radar, there was no end to the new ideas and resources that I compiled. This book is a practical guide relating what I have found out so far. I'll show you how I used that information to transform our culture at PeopleG2 and, from that effort, to transform our prospects in a competitive market.

I realized that this was something I should have been doing from day one, and that evaluating and fostering company culture should be an ongoing effort. Without this strong foundation, any small business or corporation will be more vulnerable during challenging times. My approach was, and still is, to analyse the best work cultures, and to extract not only the most novel best practices, but those that pop up in great cultures again and again. For, the more I looked, the more I noticed a pattern to both success and failure. I thought that, armed with this information, many shaky enterprises could right themselves and become prosperous.

So, again, I took to writing, but not with dry-erase markers. In Part 1 of *The Power of Company Culture*, I show business leaders and HR professionals how to spot tears in the corporate fabric before they unravel beyond repair. I note the foundations of good culture, such as opportunities for the workforce to enjoy some degree of: autonomy in making judgement calls and reaching objectives; mastery in their areas of strength; and a guiding purpose for doing the work that they do for an enterprise of which they are a part. I also show you how to determine where your company stands in those areas, as well as others that will shape your company's image and environment. Evaluating where you are now will show you how to plan a cultural makeover, step by step.

In Part 2, I offer seven pillars of effective workplace culture, which collectively provide a model for success. They are:

- Transparency
- Positivity
- Measurement
- Acknowledgement
- Uniqueness
- Listening
- Mistakes (yes, *mistakes*)

It may be that you are strong in most of these and missing only one or two crucial elements. You can customize your approach to make these your priorities. Here is a quick pillar checklist:

I: Transparency. Transparent organizations encourage the company-wide flow of communication and information, which can range from simple employee feedback to sharing profit and loss statements. Greater transparency brings together individuals and teams, putting everyone on the same page in forwarding the company's mission and vision. This is a proven strategy for enhancing performance and retaining talented employees.

II: Positivity. Much is made of problem solving, but new, positive approaches to facing stark realities, challenges and projected outcomes build on company *strengths* rather than weaknesses. This allows team members to neutralize or put into perspective so-called problems, allowing staff to gain rather than lose ground to setbacks. If your company always seems to be on the defensive, waiting for the next problem to arise, adopting a positive mindset will stoke morale and help you get out from under a negative or fearful cloud.

III: Measurement. There is no better way to gauge business performance than through the process of gathering information, measuring it and analysing it. Whether it is quantitative or qualitative, objective or subjective, data is out there for the taking. Tracking profits, losses, customer satisfaction, employee engagement, objectives achievement – or whatever metric tells you how your business is doing – lets you make informed decisions. You can even measure internal performance in each of these pillar areas to reveal opportunities for cultural improvement.

IV: Acknowledgment. The ways in which your company recognizes and rewards outstanding work are visible links in the cultural chain that binds together your workforce. Research shows that it is the act of acknowledgement, not the value of the reward, which motivates people. Great corporations choose highly visible ways of saying thank you to their employees, because observing the interaction is as important as being the giver or receiver. This is another vital culture builder.

V: Uniqueness. From individual diversity to product or service selling points, the unique aspects of any company distinguish its brand. An ability to recognize and appreciate uniqueness in prospective talent – and to understand which traits will apply to which positions – are marks of a great HR team. People who feel well suited to their jobs tend to stay, thrive, and add to great culture.

VI: Listening. In successful business transactions, listening is an active, not a passive, skill. Creating a culture that fosters active, results-based listening can set your company above the competition. Internally, staff gain a deeper understanding of projects and initiatives, for more accurate or effective results. Externally, vendors and clients feel valued and glad to continue the relationship with your company. Listening well requires a conscious effort and company-wide commitment, further bringing your team together.

VII: Mistakes. How companies deal with failure, not success, is the better marker of great culture. This pillar highlights the culture spectrum. Organizations that seek to control and punish members for making mistakes have unwelcome atmospheres, revolving-door staff and poor morale. Those that use poor outcomes as learning experiences encourage innovation and mutual respect. Their employees often far exceed expectations when allowed to try and fail.

For each of these pillars of success, I will relate what is at stake and what the payoff will be. You will find scientific research, company profiles and personal experiences that illuminate each concept, and advice on how to implement policies and protocols.

Part 3 of this book is full of proactive ways to put your programme together and get it off the ground. Generating buzz and bringing management and staff on board will pave the way towards achieving new cultural heights in your organization. Whether you focus on one or two pillars, or raise them all, in succession, you will see noticeable, positive change. You will be able to feel it in the way your people interact, and you can measure it in cash saved and greater revenues collected.

It all starts with putting your finger on the pulse of your company's culture and considering how you can make it healthier. PeopleG2 has evolved in ways that never would have been possible had I not taken a step back for a hard look at how we communicate, and how we make our decisions. Now I embrace that sort of self-evaluation. It is part of our business plan.

Perhaps most important in the coming chapters, I will discuss the downs as well as ups, and the learning experiences that spark new ideas. My story, with its twists and turns, shows that the way forward in business is not always clear. But, sooner or later, the fog lifts and the sun shines.

PART ONE
Where to start

Foundations 01

It is fascinating how some principles of business apply only to those in certain sectors and how some have universal applications. That does not mean we cannot learn from all kinds of transactional styles. If I hadn't done so back when I was looking for a way out of business collapse during the 2009 US economic downturn, I would not have a company today, let alone a book. Good times come and go. My goal is to help readers build the type of structural foundation that helps businesses weather storms and take advantage of the sunshine.

Let's start by doing some homework. I have pulled together the characteristics that are proven to move businesses forward, as evidenced by the real-world track records of top companies. Throughout this book, you will see what worked for them, as well as for my company, PeopleG2, in our mission to provide employment screening and background checks to other businesses. Sift through these examples and choose what best suits you. But be sure to pay attention to the markers of bad company culture, which by themselves can bring down an enterprise. Before we get to the distinction between the good, the bad and the ugly, let me share my method for evaluating business performance and tracking which elements of culture appear to drive it.

Once I latched on to the certainty that how we interact at work and how we do business bears on our success, it was fairly simple to find good corporate benchmarks. We know the top companies, they are vocal about their culture, and we have ready resources to find out more. These corporations typically tell everyone what they are doing and how they are doing it, in books, articles, case studies, webinars, and any other way they can get their message out. Yes, it is great publicity for their products or services. But it also builds brand credibility and attracts the best people. By sharing with the world in an altruistic fashion, these businesses are also ensuring that top job candidates know what their companies are all about.

So, I went looking. Some of the best companies that I studied included Google, Costco, 3M, Zappos, Apple, Edelman, General Motors, Amazon, Warby Parker, Southwest Airlines, Nike, Facebook and Adobe. Along the way, I read about and studied hundreds of other establishments whose products and services you might use every day. How did they remain competitive? What makes them unique?

Analysing the best and worst companies

Let's back up to my starting point. Before hosting my radio show, and before my interest in culture had become an obsession, I had to take that first step to solve my own problem. At PeopleG2, sales were down, morale was even lower and we were fighting to survive. We needed role models. One of the first places I went looking was Google, the internet technology giant. It was easy to admire the beanbag seating, employees riding scooters in the halls and enjoying free meals, and the over-the-top visual persona that the company exudes. Yes, Google made its work environment attractive. But what was the result? Better yet, what were the vehicles to that virtual destination?

Google's Laszlo Bock, senior vice president of People Operations, graciously shared those secrets in his 2015 book, *Work Rules!*[1] He had spent a decade developing human resources culture at Google. He described three catalysts to that evolution:

1 Finding a compelling mission.

2 Being transparent.

3 Giving their people a voice.

That sounds really cool. But, what does it mean? How do you do that? What if you're not Google (ie lacking brand sexiness or warehouses full of cash and resources)?

I still had some thinking to do before I could understand how to apply concepts from one business sector to success in another. Maybe Google was too unique, I worried. They had all kinds of free rein to build culture their way – with the brilliant people they had, loads of cash and programmers, and their supermodel good looks. I tried to imagine what would happen if I let people ride around in scooters at PeopleG2, flying by my office on their way to the bathroom. That would not have worked. I needed to find a way to translate their example into how we could develop our own culture, in our own way.

As I analysed other top companies, it was apparent that *they* had done much of their best work in *their* own way. Yet patterns emerged. In studying hundreds of top companies on my own, surveying HR professionals and

C-level leaders, and having deep conversations with many of them on my radio show, certain truths kept appearing. Seeing the same broad concepts was exciting; however, noticing how specific cultural components can vary company to company *or* can be customized, was even more exciting.

I had hit upon a treasure trove of information. All I had to do was correctly interpret it. The immediate question I had to answer was, 'Is this true for the biggest and best only, or is it true for all companies?' I gained the context I needed to evaluate culture over time as I interviewed professionals from companies of diverse sizes, locations and offerings.

Still, I realized that studying only the best would not tell me enough about broken culture, and why that can drag down otherwise promising businesses. I also needed to provide some sort of scale against which other entrepreneurs could evaluate their own internal operations. So, besides looking at the superstars, I had to find some poor performers, as well as some truly awful companies. Further, I would need to link their status to their working culture, and to rate them across the spectrum of good, bad and ugly. Fortunately, we live in a world in which analytics rule.

I'm not alone in grading the performance of prominent businesses. Two respected sources for this effort are *Fortune* and *Inc.* business magazines, which publish their own findings each year. The 'Fortune 1000' list focuses on annual revenue to rank the 1,000 highest-grossing public and private firms. The 'Inc. 5000' list tracks the top tier of privately held enterprises that are experiencing the fastest growth, based on three-year revenue trends.

My working assessment pool included 10 Fortune 1000 companies, about 100 Inc. 5000 companies, and another 100 unlisted companies local to my Southern California headquarters. It was easy to identify the key players that were doing well. Profits are a great yardstick and, to some extent, reflect good company culture. In order to contrast the good guys with the companies that might be struggling, I also studied staff retention versus turnover, and customer and employee satisfaction.

Some of my sources for this more intimate and subjective information included the Better Business Bureau, and business review websites such as Yelp and Glassdoor. Yelp allows any users to post their personal experiences and assessments of local businesses online. Glassdoor publishes anonymous reviews of specific businesses, made by employees who work or have worked there. Their insights and ratings proved valuable in linking culture with a company's business standing.

Looking at the revenue numbers and comparing personal accounts of businesses by clients and employees allowed me to gauge companies' success. Then, studying how those companies conducted internal and external business revealed commonalities among their culture that naturally divided into good, bad or ugly classifications. I considered great revenue and low turnover numbers to be indicators of success. Businesses that could claim those metrics, in light of my research, tended to have good culture, and the opposite was true: the struggling companies shared common traits of bad or ugly culture.

You are probably already aware of how successful or challenged your company is in market performance. Where does your company fall on the culture scale? Here are some hallmarks to watch out for.

Signs of good culture

Suppose you wanted to start a homeowner's association. You might begin by assembling a group of residents and agreeing on what you want to accomplish – say, to maintain attractive amenities and to keep vacancies and disputes at a minimum. You would want to codify these points, so you would issue standards, rules and protocols. So it goes with creating business culture. Great culture doesn't just happen. The best examples of it are premeditated, monitored and open to discussion.

In the planning stages, most businesses create guidelines for what they want to accomplish and how they will do it. If yours hasn't done so yet, set up some strategy meetings, put heads together and issue these foundational goals:

- values statement;
- mission statement;
- vision statement;
- customer service focus.

These should express where your company is coming from and where it wishes to go. Clients and the general public may or may not ever see these guidelines. Their true purpose is to form a baseline understanding for staff members – at every level – of the company's *how* and *why*. Only by working from points of agreement can a workforce pull together.

We will talk more about these crucial statements in a moment. Once they become part of the company record, though, don't sweep them under the rug. Keep them in the working lexicon to keep everyone on the same page. It is well known that, not only does Google have great culture, people there talk about it all the time. Your company's values and priorities should be so well enunciated that each manager and employee can name them – and be prepared to adapt them, if necessary. The company ethos may need to change to meet new challenges or opportunities. To enable a dynamic, shared working philosophy, communication must be continually encouraged within company ranks.

How?

Here are some examples of how businesses with good culture do it.

Values statement

What is the difference between a company's values and its mission? Values are criteria used to make business decisions, while a mission is the desired result of those decisions. Too often, I see mediocre or failing management teams push everything into either a values or a mission statement. Separating these two different concepts is, first, a clarifying exercise. Then, any company member can use the values statement as guidance in policy meetings, interviews, departmental reviews and other interactions with employees, vendors and customers. Company values become the underpinnings for making decisions that will *forward* the company's mission.

So, what is a values statement? It is an expression of an organization's philosophical beliefs, from which – not coincidentally – a common culture develops. The pronouncement can be short or long, in prose or list form. Perhaps the most concise example comes from Adobe Systems, a well-known computer software company:

'Genuine. Exceptional. Innovative. Involved.'[2]

Four stand-alone words create the context needed to understand what drives Adobe's decisions and actions. You can see that a great deal of thought went into this model, because it speaks directly to judgement calls that the company's people will have to make:

- **Genuine**: want to know how to act with fellow employees? Wondering how to speak with that difficult client? This is clear-cut. Be genuine or, as the company website goes on to define that, be 'sincere, trustworthy and reliable'.
- **Exceptional:** 'Committed to create exceptional experiences that delight our employees and customers.' If you have ever used Adobe's Photoshop

program or seen some of the amazing things that artists come up with, this statement is perfect. Note that the work should engage Adobe's employees as much as the product should make customers happy.

- **Innovative:** what the company does should involve matching 'new ideas with business realities'. Spurred by this value, Adobe went from making graphic design software – such as Photoshop and Acrobat – to creating functional file formats for documents (the PDF) and web, video and audio editing programs. Without innovation as a core value, Adobe would be a far different company.

- **Involved:** this value promises equally attentive engagement with 'customers, partners, employees and the communities we serve'. The upshot is accountability across the board. The implied vehicle? Communication.

Mission statement

This goal-oriented definition of what a company strives to *do* is often over-processed, which may be a sign of an ambiguous business focus. What does your company do primarily? Can you answer that in one sentence? Your mission statement should be easy to remember, simple to repeat and clear to anyone who see or hears it.

Here are two models of succinctness, TED and the Humane Society. TED is an online technology, entertainment and design conferencing platform that features videos by experts in those and other fields. These people are passionate about their topics and seek to ignite others' interest. If you have ever watched a TED talk, you know this mission statement is right on the money:

'Spread Ideas.'[3]

This mission statement has two words. *Two words*. Everyone remembers it. TED staff and speakers all get it and act on it. The audience gets it and is encouraged to pass along the new ideas that they find.

Another concise mission statement comes from the Humane Society of the United States, a nonprofit animal welfare advocate:

'Celebrating Animals, Confronting Cruelty.'[4]

Let's say you had never heard of the Humane Society and were unaware of their outreach benefitting 100,000 animals each year. Just by reading this mission statement, you learn their primary goal and constituency.

Vision statement

Unlike a company's decision-making philosophy or actionable goals, a corporate vision describes the *result* sought from that ethos and mission. In a best-case scenario, what do you hope your business transactions will accomplish in the wider world? Here are two good examples, one from Oxfam, a poverty-relief organization, and one from IKEA, a home-furnishings retailer:

> Oxfam: Our vision is a just world without poverty. We want a world where people are valued and treated equally, enjoy their rights as full citizens, and can influence decisions affecting their lives.[5]

> IKEA: At IKEA our vision is to create a better everyday life for the many people. Our business idea supports this vision by offering a wide range of well-designed, functional home-furnishing products at prices so low that as many people as possible will be able to afford them.[6]

These two organizations set a clear tone for what they want the future to look like. It is also clear that everyone would love to see these visions become reality. A just world without poverty? Of course! Well-designed furniture we all can afford? Awesome! Besides adding credibility and integrity to their public images, these vision statements also serve to give employees a reason to get out of bed in the morning.

I've noticed that vision statements tend to be a big-company 'thing'. Many mid-level and most small businesses do not have a vision statement. The visionary concept of the company or organization might be tucked away in the founder's or leader's brain, or it could be known to a select few staff members. If your company could be more productive and you don't have this defining statement, that definitely needs to change. When employees know *why*, they are much more invested in *how* to get things done.

Customer service focus

Making the customer your top priority seems like common sense, and many managers assume that everyone knows it and works with the customer in mind. Actually *doing* the things necessary to prioritize the customer within your company day after day is not so easy. Details and diversions get in the way. Failing to anticipate all the ways in which corporate communications and service interactions bear on the customer experience can cripple the effort to satisfy clients. A written list of customer service principles can help. This will offer any remaining tactical advice that is not covered by guidance from the values, mission and vision statements. Some general examples seen over and over again in top companies include:

- Be honest: it's okay to say you don't know.

- Be empathetic: make an effort to show you care and understand.

- Value time: the more quickly you resolve an issue, the happier the customer will be.

- Make a human connection: if an automated prompt could have helped, the customer would not be relying on you.

- Listen: make sure you hear what customers are saying – and what they are not saying – about an issue.

- Be a product or service expert: relaying correct information is a big part of solving problems.

You can use surveying or brainstorming to come up with your clients' main concerns. In Chapters 4 and 5 see the suggestions for determining how key performance indicators impact customer service and how client surveys impact performance. Then, it is up to your management team to keep these fresh in every employee's mind and to see that they act on them.

Top-down communication

Open and inclusive communication is the final shared foundation of good company cultures. There are two general types of communication within an organization: those that flow down the chain of command, and those that flow up.

Let's start with those that flow down. This style is the most common and usually exists to some degree in every company or organization. How extensive are your internal missives from the top? Does your CEO regularly send out a company-wide e-mails updating the entire workforce on a new direction? Is someone talking about good news or bad news on a large scale? What about training webinars, sales updates or a company newsletter? These are good examples of baseline information coming from the top. As this book unfolds, we will get into the details of how to issue relevant and unifying communication from management's perspective.

The irony in top-down communication is how necessary it is, and how so many companies do not execute it properly. When done right, it allows leaders to point the company ship in the right direction. In Steven Covey's must-read book, *The 7 Habits of Highly Effective People,* the author writes: 'Management is efficiency in climbing the ladder of success; leadership determines whether the ladder is leaning against the right wall.'[7] Good leaders identify need-to-know information, set it in relevant context and get it out to their teams. Leadership is not the sole job of the CEO; if everyone who is labelled management in your company is not doing this regularly – even if it is just once a year – your culture may look good but will not stand the test of time. Remember, ping-pong tables and free pizza add to company culture, they don't create it.

Bottom-up communication

Many companies overlook the need for feedback from employees, either because management presumes they are doing everything right, or because if they are not, they don't want to hear about it. Keeping lines of communication open between staff and upper management is not about laying blame but has twofold value. This tactic is a conduit to new ideas that only the people 'on the ground' might devise, and it is a sign of respect for the intellect and well-being of those who draw a pay cheque.

I will have specific examples in later chapters about the many ways that my company, PeopleG2, makes this type of communication a priority. But one of the most prevalent ways to get feedback from employees back up to management is the annual survey. This can be an effective, personalized tool that captures individual insights, or a bloated, multiple-choice questionnaire that wastes people's time. It is worth doing some research or hiring a consultant to find the best way to evaluate how your staff is feeling, where their challenges lie and how you might make improvements.

Other opportunities can come from one-on-one meetings, performance reviews and team conferences – and they don't have to happen by invitation. Employees themselves often overlook the softer opportunities to express their views, such as team meetings or casual lunches. They typically focus on the formal requests for their opinions. By all means, hit them with annual surveys and ask for formal reports. But look for new avenues to make their voices heard. The greater the effort that the management makes to listen, the more valued the staff will feel, and the more eager they will be to share ideas and experiences that can help the company move forward.

Signs of bad and ugly culture

If working directives and two-way communication are signs of good culture, their partial use or absence point to 'bad' – or worse, 'ugly' – company culture. Bad and ugly cultures also show similar negative traits, to different degrees. These include damaging internal narratives, hostile working environments and high turnover of employees. Such grave problems cost the company, first in productivity and second in capital. So, we also find these companies low in the rankings, or out of the running, on the *Fortune* and *Inc.* revenue-based lists.

What happens when many of these businesses try to correct their errant courses? They overcompensate, exacerbating the above problems and tanking their workforces. The best way to escape a bad company culture? Leave.

The result of damaged communication lines and obstructive work environments are high turnover rates. Note that some businesses naturally have high turnover for other reasons, such as seasonality, competitiveness in a specialized field, or dangerous work conditions. Some workers change jobs for personal reasons. This type of job turnover is termed 'voluntary' and it occurs less frequently than the 'nonvoluntary' incidence of employees leaving their positions. The online blog Compensation Force posted a 2015 study of 28,000 organizations that determined the average voluntary turnover rate to be approximately 11.6 per cent.[8] The overall average turnover rate, including nonvoluntary, was 16.7 per cent. Here is a breakdown of those findings:

- All industries   16.7%
- Banking and finance   19.1%
- Health care   18.9%
- Hospitality   25.9%
- Insurance   12.2%
- Manufacturing   14.8%
- Not-for-profit   15.7%
- Services   14.9%
- Utilities   9.0%[8]

In doing my company rating research, businesses that exceeded average turnover became possible examples of bad or ugly cultures. As I dug deeper, I found one big motivation-killer for the average employee to do their job, and to keep doing it: a restrictive work atmosphere.

Too much control

Companies that start out with too many restrictions on employees may see them leave in higher than typical numbers. In reviewing HR management practices, I was shocked at the volume of time, space and paper wasted on regulating things such as lunch breaks, holidays, work hours, communication formats, dress code and other behaviour-conforming rules. In an effort to fix their own errors, they may mistake control for good business practices. They might add new rules and restrictions, and assemble a team of enforcers. The resulting negative, toxic energy drains the well-being of the company and limits what it can do for customers, vendors and the community. Soon, 'command and control' becomes the default management style.

How does it work? And how does it contribute to poor company culture?

First, someone with authority creates a rule or practice to enforce a desired outcome, without any input from those impacted by the rule. This type of disenfranchisement relegates workers to toddler status, demanding that they 'do what I say, because I said so'. But employees are not toddlers. They don't surrender like toddlers eventually do when they are too tired or powerless to fight back. Instead, they act like teenagers – wiggling around the rules, finding loopholes, being passive-aggressive, or flat-out defying authority and begging for a confrontation.

The irony is that none of this is necessary. Companies with good culture find ways to empower employees to make correct decisions themselves, rather than having to be reined in by management. Many restrictions in the workplace are superfluous to doing a good job.

Labouring under unnecessary rules is bad for morale, which is bad for motivation to perform, which is bad for... company culture. Sure, if your people work on an assembly line and everyone depends on the next co-worker in line to get the job done, then it makes sense to schedule floor hours and breaks at the same time. For less interdependent office workers, though, who cares if they want to take lunch at 11 o'clock instead of noon?

Often, the real problem does not arise from the employees as a group – it is that the individual hiring went poorly, and management failed to correct it. Maybe they erroneously selected someone whose skills or work ethic did not match the company's values, mission, vision or commitment to customers. Having brought the wrong person in to do a job, management then commands that person to conform to its ideal. To avoid taking responsibility for a bad hire, the honchos might dictate a long list of rules for everyone else's behaviour.

The fix would be to correct the hiring process – thoughtfully selecting the type of person who can make appropriate decisions about what to wear, when to take their lunch, and how to carry out the company's mission based on clearly communicated objectives. This brings us to another, more subtle culture breaker, which also comes from the top: neglect.

Lack of cultural support

The damage caused by failing to nurture good company culture might not be evident until a crisis occurs, such as weak sales numbers, an accident, or loss of a key client. But it is there, for sure. Lack of focus on internal relations may occur because management chooses other priorities, or because it believes its company culture is fine and runs on autopilot. The latter leaders may live in denial, thanks to having a hot product or service or a seemingly endless supply of customers. While sales are good, no one bothers to feed the culture. Into this void move employees in need of a unifying ethic, and cliques and subcultures form around those individuals who make the most noise.

So, what happens when popularity fades or markets shrink? A culture that has been operating by itself in rogue silos breaks down. Some areas may work, some may limp along, and other areas may fail. Suddenly, a once monolithic organization divides into parts of the whole. It is every employee for themselves, in an effort to protect their own interests, since no one knows exactly what the company interest is – or, if they do, they perceive it as antithetical to their own agendas. Tribes and individuals desperately protect their turf, withholding resources and information vital to the other groups. Simple examples might include doctors against nurses, teachers against administrators, teachers against other teachers, and your staff against your clients. Those pesky customers can get in the way of an otherwise pleasant work day!

Subcultures in organizations occur, and can be quite effective. However, when the overarching culture is not defined, subcultures take over, and generally not in the interest of the company as a whole. These employees set and realize their goals just to keep their jobs, or to earn a pay rise. Conversely, the best companies and organizations form teams of individuals who are motivated to freely cooperate and work outside of cliques and tribes towards the same goals.

So, how important to productivity *is* working culture, anyway? That is easiest to see in its absence. When bad cultures are at play, employees are left to freely create their own realities inside the company. They do this by adopting their perceptions and stories as truth. When something goes wrong, it is easier to believe that the people around you are doing badly than it is to admit you are ill suited to your job or are not doing your part to make things better. In later chapters, we will explore why this is so, and why humans do so much to avoid regret.

Alternate realities and circumvention of rules erode common culture, whereas shared goals and adherence to accepted standards build it up. By now, you should have the basic tools you need to identify the difference between companies whose cultures have gone from bad to ugly, and those doing culture well. The remainder of this book will serve to help you appreciate the benchmarks of good culture and implement them in your company.

How do we build good culture?

If your company is just starting out and you have the luxury of focusing on culture from the ground up, great. If not, and if you suspect your internal foundation could use some shoring up, the first step is to determine what is at risk or already shaky. Chapter 2 will help you to evaluate objectively where your company stands. Even if you consider your organization to be in the good culture club, by now you realize that circumstances change, and you should be ready to adapt from the inside out.

Chapters 3 through 9 will present the ideal cultural elements that will allow you to do that, or to excel during the good and bad times. I call these the 'seven pillars of success'. They can be used individually or in succession to form a comprehensive programme.

You will find clear and practical ways to integrate these concepts into your working culture in Chapters 10 and 11. A strong word of caution: sometimes change in one area reveals weakness in another. Culture-wise, many companies look good on the surface, but bad habits lurk just out of sight. Don't be surprised if those habits are exposed as problematic as you look to make improvements. Be prepared for some unknown issues to arise.

As you go through this book and find areas for cultural improvement, prioritize them. Use a letter, number or star system (A–B–C, 1–2–3, ***) to clarify which items are the most pressing. Then, when you are ready to enact change, there is only one place to go to get an unbelievable result: start with the bad. This suggestion comes from my personal experience. Success has always come more quickly when I tackled the areas where I felt we were the worst. This is where I see HR professionals trip themselves up repeatedly. They convince their CEO to make some small improvement because it is easy, will not be widely rejected and can give the organization a fleeting sense of accomplishment. That's great, but it leaves the heavy lifting for another day and increases the odds that it will not be addressed.

Think of it this way: you don't fix scratches when you have broken bones or internal bleeding. If you were in a car accident and were rushed to the emergency room, you would expect your doctor to stabilize the most serious injuries first. That is no time for denial. Even if your company is not headed for a metaphorical intensive care unit, there is always room for improvement. No one – and no company culture – enjoys perfect health. Companies that look robust, like Facebook and Apple, are always working on maintaining a healthy working culture. So, join the top companies, and let's get to work!

Notes

1 Bock, L (2015) *Work Rules! Insights from inside Google that will transform how you live and lead*, Hachette Book Group, New York

2 Adobe (2015) [accessed 3 April 2017] Adobe Fast Facts [Online] http://www.adobe.com/about-adobe/fast-facts.html

3 Ted (2017) [accessed 3 April 2017] Our organization [Online] https://www.ted.com/about/our-organization

4 The Humane Society of the United States (2017) [accessed 3 April 2017] About us: Overview [Online] http://www.humanesociety.org/about/overview

5 Oxfam International (2017) [accessed 10 July 2017] Our purpose and beliefs [Online] https://www.oxfam.org/en/our-purpose-and-beliefs

6 Ikea (2017) [accessed 4 April 2017] Our vision and business idea [Online] http://www.ikea.com/ms/en_AU/about_ikea/the_ikea_way/our_business_idea/index.html

7 Covey, S (1989) *The Seven Habits of Highly Effective People: Powerful lessons in personal change*, Simon & Schuster, New York

8 Compensation Force (2016) [accessed 8 April 2017] 2015 Turnover rates by industry [Online] http://www.compensationforce.com/2016/04/2015-turnover-rates-by-industry.html

Evaluation 02

For CEOs and other accomplished managers, going back to basics can be tough. Whether out of optimism or wishful thinking, we expect to move forward and never double back. But, in order to move forward, we must gauge our baseline. Where are we now? Do we need to instil, resurrect or improve our company culture? Self-evaluation, like I performed with PeopleG2, will provide the answers. In this chapter, we will explore some of those baseline areas, and asses your readiness to implement further change.

It is your turn to shine that white-hot light on the people and policies in your organization. Is your company doing the basic things that bring about and support good culture? To answer that, you will have to honestly assess internal corporate mechanics. In this chapter, I give you a few solid nuts and bolts that must be in place before you can start raising cultural pillars. Read them. If you've got them, terrific. You can move on. If not … well, you will know where to begin.

There is just one catch to this phase of self-evaluation: the root word *self*. In examining the company yourself, you run the risk of being too subjective. When I ask you to honestly judge whether you've got the basics or how solid they are, consider what that means. You may or may not like what you find. Confronting reality is difficult for many people, especially those of us in leadership positions. We are responsible for good business performance. We want to believe our companies are great and that we have done enough to keep them that way. Yet, we also know, deep down, that if we are wrong, we may fail. And we have to admit that things may change. Living in denial does not change those facts.

I did not relish looking for the demons in my company's structure, but it had to be done. One of my favourite illustrated books as a young child was *The Monster at the End of This Book* by Jon Stone, which happens to be about fearing what one might find around the corner. Its main character, Grover, a famous Sesame Street personality, implores readers not to turn the pages, as there is a monster waiting at the end of the book. Page after page, he tries to shield readers from advancing through the book, forming obstacles using rope, wood and even bricks to prevent the reader from meeting a terrible fate at the end of the story.

Unlike lovable, furry Grover, I want you to turn the pages in your company history. I want you to find the monsters lurking in meeting rooms, under desks, in the board room and in snarly e-mails. Only by shedding light on them can you subdue them. Like the readers of Stone's book, you may find that exposing them is not as frightening as it may have seemed. At the close of Grover's story, he – and his readers – realize that *he* is the monster in question ... and that he is not so bad, after all.

With this in mind, let's start evaluating company culture where I, myself, started: with some concepts about workplace motivation put forward by author and television host Daniel H Pink. Pink recaps the most important scientific research into the keys to good work performance in an entertaining animated video by the same name of his best-selling book, *Drive: The surprising truth about what really motivates us*.[1] Pink's work resonated with me because he reveals that a commonly accepted motivator – the carrot and the stick, or the theory that punishment and reward compel better performance – is more false than true. It turns out that encouraging individual satisfaction, which seems counterintuitive, is actually the better motivator – and Pink cites respected scientific studies to prove it.

Pink suggests that, instead of a bonus and penalty system, employers enact policies that allow staff three proven motivators: autonomy, mastery and purpose. The licence to work autonomously, in their own way, or to make certain decisions for themselves often results in greater innovation, as employees feel free to offer insights that may not occur to policymakers. Giving your people the chance to specialize and master certain skills, rather than working assembly-line style or performing only part of a task, keeps them continually seeking improvement – and defining an overarching purpose for what a company or staff member does is a key driver of self-motivation.

Pink notes a common thread among autonomy, mastery and purpose: they are each something that human beings naturally want and actively seek in life. Hence their motivational force. We will talk more about these three crucial pieces of cultural hardware in a moment. To them, I would add diversity, meaning diversity of thought, not different physical or social traits. I consider a diverse workforce to be one that includes a spectrum of viewpoints and thinking styles – as wide a range as possible to be relevant and effective in a given business sector. Such diversity challenges team members and maximizes a company's chances to innovate.

Taken together, these four nuts and bolts provide stability for a cultural foundation. Once they are in place, you will be able to assemble the pillars of success that I will introduce in Part 2 of this book. So, think about your company, and compare it to others for which you have worked. How well do their structures incorporate opportunities for autonomy, mastery, purpose and diversity? Let's discuss each of these aspects more fully, so you can answer that question.

The nuts and bolts of culture

Autonomy

Do you have adequate independence to do your job? Are your co-workers or employees free to set their working parameters to fulfil their job descriptions? Or does management feel the need to outline every step? The Merriam-Webster dictionary defines *autonomy* as 'the quality or state of being self-governing'.[2] In the corporate context, I take the definition a bit further. The ability to govern ourselves at work allows us not just to satisfy our job requirements, but to excel at them – yet not to exceed them. This subtle distinction may be what puts off some leaders, preventing them from trusting employees to make judgement calls. But, with advance guidance (remember those values and mission statements?), most employable adults can – and should be allowed to – call the shots at least some of the time.

Being autonomous does not mean you get to do whatever you want. It doesn't mean that a customer service representative can, on a whim, choose to switch over to sales. Autonomy at work is the flexibility to do your job the way you see fit, *within the constraints of the position.*

Here is what those fearful leaders don't understand: autonomy works when we clearly lay the boundaries for a position and allow freedom within those parameters. For employees, those boundaries provide clarity on what to do, and on what defines success. It's like giving kids a colouring book and asking them to colour inside the lines. If the result will be what you want – a pleasing piece of artwork – you don't have to tell them which colours to use when, and how hard to press down on the paper (see Figure 2.1).

Figure 2.1 Autonomy with boundaries

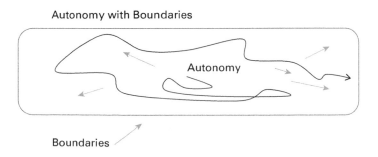

Just like kids with crayons, when employees reach a boundary and comply with it, they can choose to either work inside the organization to get things done, ask for more input, or stop, having completed the task. Following layers of rules to stay inside the lines makes colouring no fun. But being free to do what seems best within the boundaries lets the magic happen. This is what I mean about autonomy sparking creativity and innovation. It lets people *think* outside the lines, even as they stay put within them.

Just having this sort of autonomy motivates employees, and may mean more to them than a bonus. Daniel Pink's book and video reveal the seemingly contrary link between greater financial reward and job performance. The Harvard study that he followed showed that cash bonuses did improve work performance on strictly mechanical tasks, like assembly-line work. But when cognitive skills were involved, higher money incentives actually *decreased* performance. Could it be that humans value something greater than money, when it comes to work? As the researchers found and Pink articulated, yes! – autonomy being one of those things.

What happens in the opposite circumstance? Laszlo Bock gets into the pitfalls that arise at tightly controlled companies; in his book *Work Rules!* (2015) he discusses an MIT study that focused on two garment plants in Mexico. One was tightly controlled from the top, and the other self-run. Simple mathematics show which business came out ahead in that equation: the garment plant where the employees were self-directed had higher productivity and lower costs, and made more money. This was a basic comparison. Another investigation, though, published in the journal *Personnel Psychology* and funded by the University of Sheffield, confirmed that finding with a subject pool of 308 companies, tracked over 22 years. More data, same overall result.[3]

You might be as surprised as I was to learn that the carrot-and-stick management approach is not the best way to win the undying affection of workers. But I took the science and the advice to heart. At my company, PeopleG2, many of my staff can do their jobs wherever and whenever they want. We are now structured as a fully virtual workplace, which may not work for all businesses, but does for ours. The type of research my people do is not tied to a typical office location or time frame. If they get the work done accurately and on time, I don't mind if they want to arrange their work schedules around study, exercise or child care. I don't care about the *where* and *when*, or even the *how*. I only insist that tasks are done correctly, in the time expected, to the desired result.

The naysayers criticize what they see as a softness in investing in people, rather than demanding that they get with the programme. They don't realize that the investment is a means to an end – greater company success. You can invest in people and still focus on the bottom line. Consider increased profits as *your* bonus for giving people the freedom to make the decisions that impact their work – decisions that deeply matter to them and, in the big scheme of things, to no one else.

Your company's practice might fall somewhere along the autonomy scale from simple to complex. Simple autonomy leaves the order of work up to the employee. This might manifest as the freedom to answer e-mails or take lunch breaks whenever they are best suited to the individual, the company and the workflow. Complex autonomy involves greater choice. It might mean choosing, rather than being assigned, projects or team members, allowing for virtual work, or allowing for self-scheduling.

I have seen the benefits of greater autonomy in my business practice. The sceptics will need convincing that what looks like merely an emphasis on workers' happiness directly benefits the company. If you are in HR, this is the kind of case you need to make with your CEO or other management teams. Some might imagine employees or co-workers selfishly taking advantage of situations to avoid work, while others get stuck picking up the slack. This is a natural, yet mistaken, reaction. Come armed with reasons to deflect their fears. Take 10 minutes to show them Daniel Pink's video, or just have an informed conversation.

If you can get the people at the top on board, then change will come most easily. Many employees don't need convincing. In fact, involving them in the discussion and even formalizing exercises to identify how autonomy can play a larger role in job performance is a fantastic way to start your cultural revolution. It doesn't have to happen all at once. Start with simple freedoms, and move into more complex ways to give employees the reins. But, don't forget to outline boundaries with each new step. With a little practice, decisions by many individuals will actually pull your company together in tangible ways, so that everyone can see and feel the benefits.

Mastery

The concept of mastery might have disappeared from popular thought if Daniel Pink and his work had not shined a renewed light on the topic. In the Information Age, thanks to easy internet searches, we are at risk of losing our experts – those who have deeply studied a topic, painstakingly learned to play a musical instrument, or memorized favourite works of literature. Now, to get facts or even just a feel for an experience, we can Google things or use a program to facilitate our performance. In seconds, the search engine conjures up multiple sources. In minutes, I can know enough about every aspect of a topic that I could repeat it, and avoid having to internalize or master the content. I could use a program or an app to write music or literature.

This is both good and bad. Having access to more information brings clear benefits. But we are losing out on another positive experience: self-improvement. This is the payoff for mastering a topic or skill, and it is a desire that appears to be hard-wired into human nature. Perhaps it comes from the need to survive. We want to continually get better, smarter, stronger, etc. Even if we no longer need a particular skill, improving one makes us happy.

Unlike the idea of autonomy that took me a while to understand, the value of mastery was easy to comprehend. We like to learn new things and feel accomplished. Think about your leisure hobbies and activities. For example, I play guitar and write songs. I'm not a professional, so why do I practise guitar every day? I like it, and I enjoy the process of getting better and hearing the occasional applause.

Overcoming obstacles, and finding ways to get faster and better at what we do, is rewarding and fulfilling. It is, perhaps, a happy accident that such effort can accrue greater market share and revenue. So, in our roles as company leaders, we can build value in our businesses by capitalizing on this human penchant for mastering skills. It means something when a team member is the product expert, or the territory expert. Putting in eight or more hours at work takes on greater significance when we spend part of our day learning something new and getting better – and being recognized for it.

Consider how you can segment your company structure to allow employees to cultivate individual expertise. These may be large or small, technical or intuitive things. At the lower levels, clerks can master the ways to increase office recycling efforts, saving the company money and being satisfied with a positive impact on the Earth. At higher levels, you might recognize a team member who is particularly good at one of your company's greatest challenges – say, retaining your largest sales accounts – and task them with it.

Of course, not every position lends itself to mastery opportunities. What about employment in which mastery happens very fast, and there is not much new to learn? Many jobs, once learned, do not require improvement. They just need a body there to do the work. Maybe so, but there are still ways to add integrity to this situation.

First, we can provide cross-training or job shadowing inside the company. Even if employees will not get to master a new skill, giving them insights into other job titles and divisions can reinforce their sense of mastery in their current role, and expose them to options for future advancement. Second, companies can support employees' efforts at mastery in their off-hours. Experiencing this sense of accomplishment in some area of our lives brings a measure of contentment in both our home and work environments. Company leaders can channel these emotions by creating forums in which workers share their passion for personal endeavours.

One way to do this is to set up a fun meeting in which everyone reveals their mastery. Put it up on a board and celebrate it. Often, people don't realize that a pleasing hobby is actually a valuable or interesting skill that others might appreciate. You could start the exchange by handing out name tags that list people's work and play strengths, something along the lines of: 'Hello, my name is Jane. Areas of mastery: outside sales and quilting' or 'Hello, my name is Ron. Areas of mastery: criminal research and cello.' It is one way to get people talking about their strengths and enjoying recognition for them.

You could also incorporate this element into regularly scheduled meetings or birthday get-togethers. Co-workers may realize they have a personal passion in common, or they might be inspired to learn a new skill. As Pink points out in his work, the satisfaction that comes from wrestling with challenges and contributing personal talents surpasses that gained from monetary compensation. This is why pay bonuses have a motivational ceiling.

Remember, people need mastery in their lives somewhere. It makes sense to give them a boost that will, in turn, boost your business.

Purpose

Daniel Pink describes *purpose* as 'the yearning to do what we do in the service of something larger than ourselves'.[4] It is easy to see why this is a motivator. People will work without monetary reward for things like building a family, helping the sick or practising religious faith. Giving of oneself to those in need or for spiritual reasons offers a sense of hope and fulfilment. This principle may seem to have no connection to the corporate world, which, after all, exists for reasons of financial gain. But, if we look more closely, we will see where a 'higher' purpose intersects with the practical purpose of making money.

We get a healthy serving of context for this idea of purpose in the workplace from author and popular motivational speaker Simon Sinek. In his book *Start With Why: How great leaders inspire everyone to take action*,

Sinek uses the term *why* to denote *purpose*.[5] In other words, why you do something is your driving force for wanting to do it. Yes, businesses exist to make profits. But, when it comes to achieving work objectives, Sinek argues, money should never be the sole driver. It is actually a *less powerful* motivator than that amorphous sense of fulfilment we all yearn for.

In a corporate framework, think of a company's mission or vision statement as its collective 'why', one put forth by the founder or current leaders. This should have some trickledown effect to every member of the enterprise. As an individual employee, do you share the purpose expressed by the company? If not, is there some aspect of that 'why' that excites you? For instance, my company, PeopleG2, provides background checks and drug testing to HR departments, with the goal of making the world a slightly safer place. Because this is a service goal that clients value, we make money doing it. But, we enjoy a measure of pride and satisfaction in knowing that our timely and accurate work increases public safety and helps employers to make better decisions. It's that bonus of over-and-above-profit benefit that enriches our work experience and keeps us coming back for more.

Generating this warm and fuzzy feeling alone will not guarantee financial success. When combined with a good business model, however, an overarching purpose can catapult both job satisfaction and company revenues. Warby Parker, an ambitious prescription eyewear manufacturer, shows us how successful this can be. The company's 'why' – a world in which everyone can see clearly, stylishly and at affordable prices.[6] To demonstrate this commitment, for each sale it makes Warby Parker donates a pair of glasses for distribution to underserved communities. The company's 'why' is married to its revenue!

These concepts are not antithetical. As employees of Warby Parker go about their work they know that everything they do contributes to both the company's solvency and an admirable purpose. The level of job satisfaction is reflected, in part, by the company's astonishing climb in the market. Founded with start-up investments in 2010, Warby Parker grew to be worth over $1 billion in just five years, beating out the top tech giants as the 'most innovative company' of 2015.[7] Online and retail sales are helmed by the company's self-described 'team of experts',[8] who help customers find the right fit for frames. Innovative? Expert? Besides sharing a common laudable purpose, it sounds like Warby Parker's employees likely enjoy autonomy and mastery opportunities in their work.

You can see how these motivating factors help retain good talent and promote a strong work ethic, reducing costs and increasing profits. What is missing, then, from the basics on which to build your company's cultural foundation? To my mind, a deep pool of creative ideas is the final source from which a company can always draw – to solve problems, to find opportunities and to nail its stated goals. I call this openness to wide-ranging perspectives *diversity*, and it goes hand in hand with these other reasons to get up in the morning and go to work.

Diversity

How diverse in its thinking is the team your company has assembled? Not how varied are their backgrounds or ethnicities, but how varied are their approaches to the task at hand? Before you can understand how different ways of coming at a problem can strengthen your workforce, you must recognize that such diversity exists. First, let's distinguish between the commonly used definition of diversity and the one that more closely applies to building culture.

Diversity grew to buzzword status in the US business lexicon during the 1980s, when the concept of voluntarily hiring people of different minority groups – as opposed to meeting affirmative-action quotas meant to ensure equal opportunity – gained acceptance. The theory was that a more inclusive workplace, with greater representation of women, immigrants and other minorities, would provide a richer talent pool. It also served business purposes of reflecting the ethnic and gender backgrounds of its associates and clients, particularly for companies that operated globally.

This meaning falls short of mine today. An integrated workplace is a worthy goal, and an important outcome in most situations. But, from a cultural standpoint, limiting diversity programmes to target and assist particular *groups* of people excludes the individual from the equation. To me, diversity indicates a corporate structure composed of differing elements or qualities. From those *individual* qualities comes monolithic strength. Therefore, they must be qualities of mind and character. Not appearance. Not gender. Not race. Not sexual preference. Those are all important factors that allow a company to interact with neutrality, within the laws and norms of society and the local, national or global marketplace. Cultural diversity, for our purposes, is a condition that engenders self-respect as it contributes to the brain trust of an enterprise.

The distinction may seem subtle, but a focus on group diversity can actually divide and weaken a workforce, while intentional cultural diversity harnesses individual strengths. To compare the two, let's see how a short-sighted group diversity programme compares with those that boost diversity in thinking.

Uber is a US transportation company that uses online technology to increase convenience for its customers. They can request rides and transact payments through a smartphone app – no hailing a car on the street or fumbling with change. Uber's diversity profile states that reflecting the wide-ranging backgrounds of its taxicab drivers and riders is a company priority.[9] That's too bad. Had they concentrated on thought diversity, they could have avoided trouble.

The company started 2017 with a slew of scandals. Like many other cab companies, males predominate the workforce, whose racial backgrounds, in Uber's case, split at about 50 per cent white and 50 per cent nonwhite. Rumours and accusations of sexual harassment, male-dominated leadership, and an environment where the most aggressive get rewarded, went public. This hurt the brand, and even though Uber's service was in great demand and the company's presence in the marketplace grew fast, Uber logged huge financial losses.[10] It was also reported by the *New York Times*, the firing of over 20 employees over harassment, discrimination and inappropriate behaviour.[11] Just a few days later, their founder and CEO resigned.[12]

While, ostensibly, the company made group diversity a priority, its leaders chose to bring in power-hungry, cut-throat employees to drive their high-growth strategy. Their problems came, not from limiting disparate groups in their workforce, but from promoting the people who *thought* the same way. The solution to increasing diversity is not to set quotas based on gender or racial make-up. It is to search for talented people with different thinking qualities and styles. When we do that, we naturally construct a far more diverse workforce.

The question is, how can we do that? The answer is, by focusing on individual strengths.

This approach prompts companies to focus on which positive traits an applicant brings to their mission, instead of emphasizing how that person might differ from the majority. In this vein, leaders must ask what types of personal aptitude best address the job tasks at hand. For instance, at PeopleG2, we need a range of thinking styles to identify HR hiring needs, stay updated on the technologies at our disposal, perform the actual work of applicant background assessment, and many other tasks. Different assignments require different skills or mindsets, which may or may not be linked to a person's gender or ethnicity.

We take a scientific approach to evaluating people's strengths. The US research firm Gallup, Inc, has produced a definitive guide for employers, using objective, strengths-based psychology. The book and online tool *Gallup's Strengthsfinder 2.0* helps hiring teams identify and understand

34 positive personal traits compiled by esteemed psychologist Donald O Clifton. These qualities fall under four main categories of strength: strategic thought; relationship development; influence; and execution.

The *Strengthsfinder* self-survey reveals your natural strengths by measuring the degrees to which you possess each of 34 marker traits. For example, based on this questioning, I found my number-one strength to be ideation, or a facility for forming and analysing new ideas. Simply put, I enjoy taking in lots of ideas and figuring out which ones are most important to our mission. Then, our company can prioritize them, and thus heighten our efficiency and effectiveness. Ideation is endemic to my personality because I find it exciting to sort through mounds of data and to witness patterns that rise above the noise. That skill, in particular, is helping me to write this book.

I have used the *Strengthsfinder* system over the years in selecting my staff. We ask every applicant to complete the quick and easy survey to discover their five major strengths. Our managers then compare these against their own appraised strengths, to see how the prospect would fit in with the team. Does this person have an ability deemed important to operations that the rest of the staff lack? Perfect! Does this person duplicate a skill set that we already have enough of? Too bad. We'll keep their CV on file.

To understand your *company-wide* strengths and weaknesses, you can plot this information on a spreadsheet that will show you what to look for in new hires. I got this idea from my mentor, Kim Shepherd, CEO of the company Decision Toolbox. She took all of the identified strengths from the company's Gallup survey and poured them into a spreadsheet, cross-referenced by employee. Once she did that, it was easy to see where the company was flush and where it was missing strengths.

This sounded like a fairly scientific process that also emphasized individuality, and seemed like an ideal way to arrive at just the right person for a given job. So, I gave it a try at PeopleG2. To be honest, when I decided to do this, it was all about pumping up the areas where we were missing strengths. It had nothing to do with diversity. But, after about 36 interviews and 10 hires, it became clear that our new selection process had changed the balance among candidates. The applicants making it to the final cut were all quite diverse from one another and from our own majority pool.

Thanks to our analysis, we were getting talent with different backgrounds, education, hobbies and the like. They also happened to be diverse from a gender and race perspective. All I did was ask my managers to locate people whom they liked and thought would be great employees, and who had a strength that we were missing. That's it. Incorporating Donald Clifton's strengths-based psychology into what was once an entirely subjective process has made a world of difference to our workforce and our company culture.

I have shared this approach with many other business leaders, and the results have all been positive. In most places around the world, humans exist in a majority group surrounded by a minority group. The mix always includes males and females of different beliefs and social structures. I cannot control that, nor can you. But if you want to bring people into your organization who will contribute to a strong company culture, then focus on strengths – what you have, and what you need. Identify your baseline and work towards improvement in your weakest areas.

Get ready to build great culture

Use these motivators and benchmarks to lay the foundation for your company's culture. Start by getting everyone on the same page and excited about a new direction. Talk about the importance of job autonomy, and help your employees find ways to exercise this skill. Let your managers know that this measure of personal freedom not only improves the work environment but can significantly improve the company's bottom line.

In fact, use that goal to sell all of these motivators – autonomy, mastery, purpose, and appreciation of diverse thinking – and then demonstrate that financial success is only one benefit. Enhanced personal satisfaction in performing work is a benefit that cannot be measured, but that makes working for your company more attractive to the best people. To that end, encourage your staff to pursue mastery of a skill or subject, whether at work or in their private lives. This leads to a healthy balance that people naturally seek.

The same is true for identifying your company's purpose, clearly articulating why you do what you do. From this vision, individuals can secure their own higher reasons for doing the day-to-day work. Remember to communicate these personal and shared goals. Every employee, vendor and customer should be aware of this all-important 'why'.

Finally, focus on the strengths that your company has and still needs by using some standard mechanism to understand your workforce. Instead of hiring people who will fall in line with what your current staff already represent, hire those who will help you fill in the gaps. Focus on diversity of thought. You might have a few more arguments in the conference room, but your staff will be better able to make decisions that are not only good for them, but will forward the company's goals and growth.

After you have evaluated your existing situation, read on. Part 2 of this book will give you the large building blocks that must rise from your company's foundation in order to erect a solid culture. Now that you know that strong culture powers strong performance, you will see why I call the following elements the pillars of success. Some of them are more complicated than others to pull together, so feel free to work on them in the order that best suits your company. The operative word here is *work*, so get ready. Take notes and roll up your sleeves. We have broken the ground. Now let's raise the structure.

Notes

1 Pink, D H (2010) [accessed 13 July 2017] RSA ANIMATE: Drive: The surprising truth about what motivates us [Online] https://www.youtube.com/watch?v=u6XAPnuFjJc

2 Merriam-Webster (2017) [accessed 9 April 2017] Definition Of Autonomy [Online] https://www.merriam-webster.com/dictionary/autonomy

3 Birdi, M, Clegg, C, Patterson, M, Robinson, A, Stride, C B, Wall, T D and Wood, S J (2008) The impact of human resource and operational management practices on company productivity: a longitudinal study, *Personnel Psychology*, **61**, 467–501

4 Pink, D H (2017) [accessed 11 April 2017] DRIVE: The summaries [Online] http://www.danpink.com/drive-the-summaries/

5 Sinek, S (2009) *Start With Why: How great leaders inspire everyone to take action*, Penguin

6 Warby Parker (2017) [accessed 11 April 2017] History [Online] https://www.warbyparker.com/history

7 Chafkin, M (2015) [accessed 16 July 2017] Warby Parker sees the future of retail, *Fastcompany.com* [Online] https://www.fastcompany.com/3041334/warby-parker-sees-the-future-of-retail

8 Warby Parker (2017) [accessed 17 July 2017] Measure your pupillary distance (PD [Online] https://www.warbyparker.com/pd/instructions

9 Uber (2017) [accessed 15 April 2017] How do we want Uber to look and feel? [Online] https://www.uber.com/diversity/

10 Rogowsky M (2017) [accessed 17 July 2017] Caution ahead: Uber's financials reveal staggering growth but raise many questions, Forbes.com [Online] https://www.forbes.com/sites/markrogowsky/2017/04/15/caution-ahead-ubers-financials-reveal-staggering-growth-but-raise-many-questions/#49f3ca34236e

11 Issac, M (2017) [accessed 16 October 2017] Uber fires 20 amid investigation into workplace culture, *nytimes.com* [Online] https://www.nytimes.com/2017/06/06/technology/uber-fired.html

12 Issac, M (2017) [accessed 21 June 2017] Uber founder Travis Kalanick resigns as CEO, *nytimes.com* [Online] https://www.nytimes.com/2017/06/21/technology/uber-ceo-travis-kalanick.html?mcubz=0

PART TWO
The seven pillars of culture success

Pillar I: transparency

Transparency – the open disclosure of information – is both a business ethic and a cultural element in the workplace. I rank it first among the pillars of success because it lies at the heart of every positive transaction, between management and employees, staff and vendors, and staff and clientele. It involves clear and unfettered communication and the presentation of accurate facts. Besides making customers feel comfortable in giving a company their trust and cash, transparency protects workers' integrity and businesses' legal standing.

In my organization, PeopleG2, transparency means much more than my working behind see-through glass walls, although that is an excellent metaphor for our commitment to being transparent. I make it my mission to encourage open communication at every level; any staff member has full licence to consult with any other member if they believe their insight will help solve a problem or open up an opportunity. This levels the playing field and keeps office intrigue to a minimum. I mentioned in Chapter 1 that many executives frown on bottom-up communication because they prefer not to hear what is going wrong or less than well. But this means they miss out on the good stuff too. Embracing transparency is choosing the mature route, in which we take the good with the bad, in order to learn from both ends of the spectrum.

As you consider where your company falls on the transparency scale, also think about what you could be doing better. Open up this topic for discussion at every level. You will get a tidal wave of new ideas that might not have occurred to you.

In this chapter, we will discuss: what transparency is and is not; why it is of value to every business – small or large; what it entails; and how to promote it.

What is transparency?

Many US businesses incorporate an approach to quality control popularized in the 1980s, called 'total quality management' (TQM). Its goal is to minimize waste and to maximize productivity towards the delivery of consistently superior products and services. One of the TQM techniques is to make staff aware of its tenets, often by posting them on placards in office halls and meeting rooms. Among them, you will almost always find a sign that simply states, TRANSPARENCY.

It looks so noble. But what is transparency? What does it mean for a company to *be* transparent?

Somehow, this is one area in which companies really struggle. The simplicity of the word lulls us into a false sense of security. General and business definitions for *transparency* agree on two things: an open exchange of information and the absence of secretive agendas.[1] Sounds like a healthy working atmosphere, doesn't it? Yet, it can be difficult to achieve and maintain, because transparency cannot be implemented equally across the board. Everyone does not get to know everything in most real-life business situations. While it is admirable to share data – whether nutrition information on consumer food labels or sales figures among departments – there are many legitimate reasons for being selective in imparting company details. Some information is proprietary, some is sensitive, some is personal. Some facts are not palatable enough to present to the public. For instance, hotdogs taste great, but that does not mean that every customer wants to know how the sausage is made.

This means that guidelines for information sharing and channels of communication must take into account the sender, the user and the nature of the material. Aha! The task of unmasking the corporate underpinnings just got more complicated. We will talk about what goes into an effort to increase transparency in a moment. This is a good time to mention what this effort helps companies to avoid.

It is no accident that businesses also define *transparency* by what it is not: inherent to the term is a lack of secretiveness. What ugly aspects of culture does this prevent? It is easy to start a list: favouritism, infighting, ignorance, immorality, lack of accountability. Transparent companies represent the opposite of the shady business dealer, for both those involved in the operation and those who do business with it.

To these bare bones of transparency – open yet circumspect communication, access to relevant information and an absence of hidden affairs – companies with good culture add more checks and balances. We will look at the basic and advanced steps, and how to apply them to your business, in a moment. First, let's talk about why you should want to do so ... and what the payoffs will be.

The value of transparency

If anyone knows what transparency is worth, it is Jack Stack, two-time author and CEO. His company, SRC Holdings Corporation, owns and has invested in over 60 companies, employs over 1,600 people and is believed to enjoy more than $584 million in annual sales.[2] *Inc.* magazine recognized SRC's operation as a number-one most innovative business practice, largely for its extensive 'open-book' culture. Stack's philosophy is that the more each employee knows about how a company works, the more they can do to improve what it does. We have already seen evidence that greater efficiency and quality work translate to greater profits in the right circumstances. SRC's growth shows that its transparent practice has paid off. The company's stock price has risen from 10 cents a share in 1983 to $435 at its most recent high mark.

I had the pleasure of hearing Jack Stack speak at the 2013 'Inc. 500/5000' conference in Washington, DC.[3] He described an advanced aspect of business transparency that has shown dividends at the corporate, personal and community levels: sharing company financial information internally with every member. His talk illustrated the value of his emphasis on top-to-bottom openness. 'We want to create employees who think and act like owners', he said. While some CEOs would hold cash flow and revenue statistics closely, Stack shares his with everyone concerned, from senior management down to the janitorial staff. His thinking: this makes *everyone* cost-conscious and financially literate.

Think about what those results mean.

Every member of SRC pulls together to reduce overheads. Every member feels encouraged to innovate to save money or improve practices or products. Every member feels trusted with privileged information. Every member has a stake in the revenue figures that they review, since SRC is a wholly employee-owned enterprise. Do you think Stack's team is loyal and hardworking?

Needless to say, costly employee turnover is not of grave concern, nor are secret efforts to divert profits. But the financial benefit does not end there. 'Tie your people into the value your company creates', Stack advised.

He considers education a binding tie, as knowledge is something that employees carry with them – to their homes, their families and their community organizations. Financial acumen, in particular, increases self-confidence and security – qualities that people value and appreciate. So, this facet of transparency, while on the complex end of the spectrum, provides great value to participants.

This example of financial openness clearly benefits the company's bottom line. But, how do the other elements of transparency – clear communication, involvement in decision making and access to information – affect *employees* and, therefore, company culture? Stack went on to enumerate these:

> **Team cohesiveness**: employees form a unified front when they are informed about how aspects of the business operate and who does what.
>
> **Dynamic leadership**: new leaders are born as employees are empowered to make decisions based on their knowledge and on the company's mission and vision.
>
> **Critical inquiry**: individuals develop greater insight about how to approach tasks as their knowledge increases and they ask tougher questions.
>
> **Knowledge dissemination**: informed employees spread the expertise that they gain on the job in their private lives and in community service, which reflects well on the company.
>
> **Employee retention**: staff members who operate autonomously and have mastery opportunities and a satisfying purpose are motivated to stay with the company. (Where have we heard that before?)

When your company becomes more transparent, suddenly the quality of your workforce and the results of their efforts grow more sophisticated and profitable. All of the above things happen when we afford employees clarity and context for what they and their co-workers do during the workday. How do we do that? By communicating. But, as anyone who has ever been misunderstood by a significant other knows, we do not always perfectly express ourselves – and those listening do not always hear exactly what we are trying to say.

Clarity in communications

The value of clear communication is evident when you realize that a single missed chance to accurately convey company information can cause a lost sale, an accident or even a lawsuit. So, it is in our best interests to know how the human mind transacts information exchanges. We're not robots. We come equipped with different points of view and learning styles, and different ways of perceiving problems and solutions. In other words, we don't always think logically when we talk, look and listen.

I got a quick lesson in these common communication hurdles one day with my son Dmitri and daughter Luba. It is called a **cognitive bias**, and I experienced it during a visit to the San Diego Safari Park in California. We were fortunate to see a special animal presentation in which a biologist brought out a jerboa, a small mammal that is native to hot climates in Africa and Asia. This comical creature has long ears like a rabbit, and muscular hind legs and a long tail like a kangaroo. Before telling us more about this unusual animal, the handler asked the group of adults and children what they thought it was.

No one could answer her with certainty; everyone took guesses. Most thought that the jerboa must be related to a rabbit, a kangaroo, or both. One boy opined that the animal's father was a kangaroo and the mother a rabbit. This prompted some jokes from the adults. Then our host said the simple sentences that would change for ever my perspective on how we perceive information: *'This animal is neither a rabbit nor a kangaroo. In fact, it is not related to either one of those.'*

She then explained our trouble in trying to identify it. Humans, she said, can use only the information at their disposal to explain something new. They cannot, or do not, consider information they do not yet have in order to judge something they have never seen before. In other words, we saw rabbit ears and kangaroo legs and made our final choices. Everyone was wrong. The jerboa is actually a rodent that evolved its features over time to outwit predators in the desert.

I was stunned. How could I have assumed something based on so little information, without any concern for being right? This troubled me for weeks. Finally, I gave up and accepted that it was human nature, or more precisely, human biology. My only defence was to be aware of how limited our perceptions can be, and to dig deeper before making conclusions. I also realized that, to limit misinterpretations on the other end, it was important to give people as much information as possible when it counted – to be transparent.

Understanding cognitive biases can help us better communicate and manage relations with our employees and other business associates. It gives us a reason to take care and communicate clearly, in a manner that best serves the listener – or at least, to notice when we have fallen short. Relaying as much relevant material as we can will reduce the chance of bad assumptions. Becoming sensitive to the learning and communication styles of others will help us know *how* to get our message across.

Of course, we don't communicate solely with information. Our tone of voice, body language and word choice continually send out cues that may support or contradict our actual words. One thing to remember is that humans process information based on an emotional filter. Logic takes a backseat. So, we need to take into account what the listener might infer: *Is he angry with me? Does she really care about my problem? Could this get me fired?*

Emotions in decision making

Author and Professor of Neuroscience, Psychology and Philosophy at the University of Southern California Antonio Damasio helps us make sense of this cognitive trait in his book *Descartes' Error: Emotion, reason, and the human brain* (1994). Damasio holds that, rather than counteracting logic, emotion plays a valuable part in aiding perception and decision making. Think back to early humans. Physical danger, hunger and the need for shelter were far greater worries then they are today. So, we developed an innate impulse to recognize emotion – say fear or discomfort – first, and to act second.

This is nice to know when you have got a dubious client on the line or you get the feeling that a business deal is too good to be true. But try telling a high-powered executive that his or her proposal comes from a personal preference rather than cold, hard data. When I ask a group of CEOs if their decisions are rational or emotional, they always say that decisions are rational. That is when I start quoting Damasio. 'When emotion is entirely left out of the reasoning picture', he writes, 'reason turns out to be even more flawed than when emotion plays bad tricks on our decisions.'[4] For some reason, we want to believe that our decisions are rational. But, we are not wired to absorb a list of facts and objectively make up our minds. We tend to make our decisions emotionally and then justify them with reason.

Our only weapon in this confusing human experience is transparency. As Damasio counsels, 'Intuition favours the prepared mind',[5] which means that our ability to make quick, accurate decisions based on gut feelings *are* reliant on the right information. If our employees have the information available, they can make better decisions consistently. So, think about this when you decide which information to share with whom in your company. In some circumstances in which team members fail to make the right choices, they may simply lack the guidance or data that more senior people keep to themselves.

Conducting business always involves a series of choices. Remember the jerboa? If we realize that good conclusions stem from possessing enough relevant information – and that poor choices can arise from limited information – then we have even more reason to communicate clearly and openly. Being able to own our decisions and project to clients that we are well informed is part of good company culture – and we owe that to the practice of transparency.

The role of mindset

While we are resolving to be more precise and forthcoming in our communications, we cannot overlook the additional cognitive bias brought on by, well, *bias*. Presumptions of mind that we form over time help us take short-cuts in thought. We don't have to judge every situation when we deem it to be 'like' other situations. We don't have to make calls on every choice when we rely on guidance that has proved useful in the past.

For instance, suppose a friend asks to borrow money that they fail to repay. The next time they need a loan, you will probably say no. Or, suppose you find a movie you're interested in watching, but a favourite critic suggests steering clear of it. You would probably give it a pass. The only problem with these preconceived notions, although they are based on previous evidence, is that they may not apply to the current situation. Your friend might have repaid with interest to make up for the last time, and might even throw a client referral your way; and while the movie critic may not have liked that film, there may have been a personal draw for you that you will never get the chance to enjoy.

Mindset expert and Stanford University Professor of Psychology Carol S Dweck helped me to understand how preconceptions can inhibit our interactions with clients and employees to a company's detriment. In her book *Mindset: The new psychology of success*,[6] she makes the distinction between what she calls a 'fixed' and a 'growth' mindset. We might have one or the other, or we might entertain both attitudes at different times. She describes how these outlooks affect the ways in which we think, talk and act.

Our mental outlook is important because it colours our reactions and our ability to reach our full potential. Dweck's research has shown that people with a fixed mindset believe their capabilities are fixed, and they are less likely to flourish. They may also believe that those around them have limited ability as well. Alternatively, people with a growth mindset believe their talents can be developed, and so they have an impetus to pursue improvement.

That is powerful. How did she arrive at this theory, and what outcomes prove it? The examples in Dweck's book regarding research with school-children were the most relevant for me. They evoke many of the training scenarios occurring inside companies every day. Some of the data was surprising. For example, an overestimation of a child's intellect could actually hinder learning. Dweck found that children who were told that they were smart after getting a good grade on a test were less likely to take risks or learn other challenging things. 'You are smart' triggers a fixed mindset. Why bother studying more advanced concepts? Trying something difficult and failing, the child might worry, would change the teacher's perception of them as smart. Could there be another way to praise a student's performance without running into this problem?

Yes. Dweck tracked what happened when teachers told students who did well on a test how hard they must have worked. 'Good job', they might say. 'Your studying really paid off.' This, she found, threw the kids into a growth mindset for the next test. These students were more likely to tackle new material and take the initiative to learn more.

These results made me ask, what messages could we be sending to our staff that enforce a fixed mindset? Sometimes just passing judgement walls people in: *This team performs well. That manager is tough. The East Coast office is filled with slackers.* The people who hear this then act on these preconceived notions, whether they are universally true or not.

After reading Dweck's book and having discussions with my staff, we discovered that people in our organization did, indeed, have some biased ideas. It became clear that all of us were probably guilty of believing something inaccurate about a person or a situation, based on some fixed mindset we had picked up. We then went on to make judgements and decisions accordingly, often with unwanted consequences.

In one instance, a group of us agreed that a certain client was the source of more than 10 per cent of the department's customer service calls and e-mails each month. It was commonly held that this client was using a disproportionate amount of our resources, and when asked, most staff members labelled the customer 'difficult'. How do you suppose we treated that person? Even when kept under wraps, our grudging mindset probably showed through and may have provoked additional animosity.

We pulled the logs from our calls and e-mails for the previous 12 months and found that, in reality, that client's input accounted for less than 3 per cent of activity. I compared this frequency to similar clients' requests. The 'difficult' clients' were fewer! So, why did we believe this customer was such a problem?

It turned out that we'd had a few tense conversations early in setting up the account, and no reset had ever happened. We reacted with mistrust and probably generated the same response. While we didn't lose that account, we were totally wrong about the client. By analysing our perceptions, and providing everyone with the data, we opened up two opportunities. We gained a second chance to smooth the way with the account in question, and we learned that, after reviewing the numbers, not only was that client not a problem but that three others actually were. This allowed us to address a situation that was dragging down our productivity.

It was transparency that got us back on track. Open discussion, frank introspection and clear communication solved multiple problems. From that day on, the customer service team changed its mindset. No more fixed statements. We replaced our bad measurement system of perceptions with a more objective monthly satisfaction survey and review. We were on our way to pursuing our goal of always improving communication and forging good relations with our clients.

Ways to increase transparency

Implementing this pillar of success can be a game changer for your organization. Simply opening management's and staff's minds to the importance of transparency will point towards the right steps for your company. Start by asking these basic questions:

1 Does everyone in the company know who is responsible for which tasks?

If you answered no, read on for ways to be more transparent about the roles in your company and whom to seek out in connection with them.

2 Is everyone aware of how those people operate – which personal styles and individual goals drive them? How about valuable clients? Do staff members know how best to convey information to them?

A *no* to these questions means that your staff can use insight into how individuals communicate and how to achieve clarity with different types of people.

3 Do company meetings take place on a level playing field? Is each employee empowered to raise concerns?

If you answered negatively, your company may still be operating on a hierarchy that excludes some voices, affecting the level of autonomy and diversity of thinking allowed. Be sure to read up on new ideas for meeting protocols, below.

4 Who needs to know what? Which undisclosed information might help staff in certain endeavours?

If there is a weak link in your company's supply chain of information, you might have a hard time answering these questions. If so, read on for ways to rethink your need-to-know calculations and how to get quality intelligence out to your people.

All of the above issues offer opportunities to increase transparency in your business practice and strengthen your company's culture. Here are some suggestions to get you started.

Understanding roles and goals

If a team is to be effective, people who work together should know a great deal about each other. The truth is that many co-workers are like estranged neighbours; they talk about the weather but never really engage in personal details. This makes for a disconnect in the company fabric. Understanding the roles and goals of co-workers mends such rifts and contributes to a more closely knit team.

I love to get a group of people together in an organization and ask them to write down what they think each person in the room does in their job, day to day. What are their roles? What are their goals in making the company successful? Once they are done, we take turns sharing a few examples for each person. They are always inaccurate.

Aside from the basic things we might guess about anyone from their job title, the guesses are completely off base. There are some chuckles and looks of exasperation among team members as the truth comes out. Then comes the fun part. To get deeper into the topic, I ask each person to describe their *own* role and up to five things that are mission-critical goals for them. Now the response from their co-workers is amazement and shock. 'I had no idea you did that!' is something we are bound to hear.

How is this possible? We spend more time with people at work than we do with our families, friends and casual acquaintances. Yet those with whom we work may know less about what goes on right alongside them than they do about the habits of their hairdresser or the salesperson at the convenience store.

By setting aside time to share information about what different people do in different company positions, you can increase the collective IQ of your organization. Understanding how responsibilities break down by department makes every staff member 'company literate'. People now know who to go to, quickly, in a time of need. They also know who requires specific data or communications as situations arise. Customer service representatives can direct client inquiries to the right person. Staff members know who to copy on that e-mail, or who needs to be in a meeting to ensure that the whole team is on board.

But, beyond what each employee does, it is helpful to know *why* they do it – how a task furthers a position's, or department's or the company's goals. This aspect of transparency relates to the beneficial cultural element of autonomy. When we know why we should do something, it increases our motivation. In this case, when we know why a co-worker does something – whether to achieve a sales goal or to get a report out before a big conference – we understand how we can help, or we at least recognize their contribution.

Being transparent about our goals affords this type of clarity and offers each person a path to success and the support of their peers. Besides providing those motivators, knowledge of roles and objectives helps identify and eliminate any overlapping or incongruent goals between staff. Suppose the vice president (VP) of marketing was charged with expanding the company's influence into one market, and the VP of sales was concentrating on ramping up sales in a totally different sector. The two executives need each other to be successful. If they don't know what the other person is trying to accomplish, how can they succeed? It is easy to see how this type of energy drain can hamper a company's success.

Yet, so many businesses struggling with culture seem to hide goals, and discourage sharing and collaboration. Is it because there is never enough time to bring new hires up to speed, as they deal with a revolving-door staff? Taking the time to be proactive in addressing this transparency issue may actually decrease the time and money spent on employee turnover. Talking about their jobs is something that everyone likes to do. So, incorporate role-and-goal exchanges into meetings, trainings, or even casual lunches. You're sure to see boosts in efficiency and teamwork.

Communicating on a personal level

Company-wide transparency clearly facilitates a better understanding of individual contributions to the company's mission and vision. But, once your employees get to know each other on a role-and-goal level, how can communications between them become most effective? We have already talked about different types of cognitive biases. How can co-workers use transparent means to bypass those roadblocks?

Suppose you are a mid-level manager trying to lead a team with diverse talents. Their problem-solving styles may be complementary, but their communication styles might be antithetical. A naturally assertive person might overshadow a more reserved speaker. A detail-oriented type might not appreciate the creativity of a big-picture thinker. Interpersonal communications can improve when those involved know more about each others' behavioural traits. Yes, this sounds clinical, but stick with me here: a simple personality assessment can lend transparency to why co-workers act the way they do – allowing all parties to adjust to accommodate each other. Company culture, after all, means that everyone is in the same boat. Like sailors, we all have to take steps to get along and make sure that all the commands are understood.

You don't have to assess every employee's personality to get insight into how different individuals behave and how best to interact with them. Choose one volunteer. Then you can talk about this subject in general terms based on the outcome of an objective assessment tool, such as one called the DISC Profile.[7] This test asks a subject to respond to a questionnaire of about 80 items, which discern how closely a trait matches their personality. Sample statements include:

- People think of me as a really good listener.
- I can be fairly forceful with my opinions.
- I love meeting new people.

The answer scale runs from *strongly agree*, *agree* and *neutral* to *disagree* and *strongly disagree*. An electronic scoring system of all answers reveals behavioural patterns and dominant traits – all of which bear on how people conduct themselves and communicate in the workplace and elsewhere.

The DISC Profile's name refers to the four main measurable traits that drive personal styles: **dominance**, **influence**, **steadiness** and **conscientiousness**. Each of these categories has typical behaviours tied to it such as a blunt speaking manner, a tendency to collaborate or a need for attention. The DISC test not only measures how people think and act, it literally reveals what to do in order to interface successfully with them. For instance, a conscientious type might appear hesitant to make a decision, but in reality is simply driven to get all the details before making a judgement call. Give them these facts, and then start talking. Or a dominant person who goes straight to the point might consider polite chit-chat a barrier to getting results. Skip the introductory words with this person and just lay out the issue at hand.

When we know these things about people we can more easily interact with them, and will be less likely to suffer misunderstandings. Team members can become more aware of each others' strengths and weaknesses, and can work together more effectively.

This testing system is popular among HR managers in all types of businesses and institutions. Many of these users keep their results private. But, revealing even a hypothetical scenario can be valuable to your company's cultural effort. I have used the DISC tool for years and find it to be spot on in its results. It's your choice; you can use any standard assessment that reveals how personality traits influence behaviour. To do so, all you need is one volunteer – yourself, perhaps – and an open forum in which to divulge what makes you tick.

I took this exercise to its extreme at PeopleG2. I sent out a note to my entire company, asking everyone to take the test that week and agree to share the results. It wasn't mandatory, but the whole staff complied because our culture allows for that kind of intimacy. This might not work in every business, but at my company, offbeat requests like this are the norm.

Enthusiasm was high among my staff, who sent their tests back to me within 24 hours. I added mine to the pile, and with this powerful data in my hands I put the results in a shared folder that everyone could access online, plus subfolders for each department. The entire company was invited to take a look. Instantly, everyone knew more about everyone else in our organization. Natural curiosity gave way to interest in the larger purpose for the exercise, and we enjoyed a bit of positive buzz for a few days. The real lightning bolts came later.

As leaders in an organization, we are in the position to mentor individuals and teams that might be struggling. Often, communication breakdown – not a lack of job know-how – is the culprit. When I sensed this problem at play in PeopleG2, we pulled up those personality test results. It turned out to be a great starting point for a useful conversation.

We have two managers who get along fine, but at first found it difficult to communicate professionally. They couldn't seem to get through to each other, and it was starting to affect the team. I sent them a computer file link, and had them read each other's profiles. Soon afterwards, one of them called me on the phone, laughing. She said she realized that she had been doing everything the report said *not* to do to reach this person. We got together, and the three of us talked over the issues that were getting in the way of understanding. They changed their approach, and things have been great ever since.

I should mention that I had to consider both managers' styles in order to confront their issue without putting them on the defensive. Their response and openness to change told me that I had done the right thing.

Find a way to discover and use this type of information with your team. Some companies simply include the DISC test as part of their onboarding process with new employees. Some keep the information confidential, and some don't. Be sure that you are clear on that point with your people. We certainly found the release of this type of information worth the privacy trade-off. For us, it was another way to leverage transparency to help make our people happier, our culture better and our operations more efficient.

Inviting input

Being transparent is not always about sharing good news. It is inevitable that someone in your organization will have to pass along disappointing or downright disastrous information to peers or, worse, senior officials. When faced with this daunting task, people may soft-pedal or openly deny the facts, tanking transparency and dealing a blow to company culture. It is not something that can be seen or clearly defined, but it weakens the foundation.

So, how can we support the delivery and acceptance of difficult news at every internal level? Perhaps part of the reason we recoil from it is that we try to avoid it. Instead, we should simply practice it.

I received great hints on how to do this from David Marquet, respected keynote speaker and author of *Turn the Ship Around*, one of my favourite books on leadership.[8] Marquet knows a thing or two about the topic, having once captained a nuclear submarine. He now advises corporations on how to use leadership principles to increase autonomy and productivity in the workplace. In 2015, we spoke on my radio show TalentTalk,[9] about how to deal with bad news and disagreeing with the group. You can incorporate his suggestions into a meeting format.

Marquet runs groups through role-playing scenarios to get them comfortable with a discomfiting chore. He first asks team members to practise giving made-up bad news to their boss. It might be about losing a hypothetical client account or relaying the need for an expensive building repair. In false situations, the employees still express nervousness and admit to having anxiety. But, practising a few times desensitizes them and increases their comfort levels.

So, Marquet then takes it a step further, in a process he calls 'designating the devil'. One or two people in the group are chosen to be the 'devil', whose job is to oppose every idea or opinion that is brought up for discussion.

In this role, they don't get to hold a pitchfork or crank up the heater, but they must steadfastly contest whatever the group's consensus is or what the boss is articulating. Essentially, they are playing devil's advocates. This gives the rest of the group the opportunity to respond to resistance and disagreements.

I liked this idea so much that I tried it at PeopleG2, and continue to do so. We choose an agenda topic to debate, and people have to adopt a pro or con stance, based on random selection. I use playing cards to decide who will be the devils. I deal them face down and instruct each person to look, but not share the identity of their card with anyone. If they get a jack, they must take the position of the devil. In the interest of letting everyone air their true views, I promise that the devils will have a chance at the end of the discussion to offer any real, positive opinions.

What happens during these meetings is nothing short of amazing. We begin discussing an issue or proposal, and the ideas start flying. Of course, the devils bring up problems and disagree with the group – but others do, too. We weave through the discourse and wind up with an agreement or next steps to take on an issue. When we finish, I ask everyone to guess who played the devil. Some get it right. Usually, they also choose someone who was *not* a devil. I love this! If the group has accepted negative opinions whether or not they were set up, it means people felt free enough to give and listen to 'bad news' with open minds.

This exercise is illuminating. Without this type of practice, people might go along with things they are not really okay with, or might hesitate to dole out negative thoughts. Transparency is not just about passing along pleasant information. It must include the freedom to express unwelcome news and alternate opinions.

Sharing financials

Let's return to the story of Jack Stack and his incredible organization, SRC Holdings. In the interest of transparency, it was Stack's idea that, not only should everyone in the company have access to financial records, they should be trained in how to understand them. If you have ever seen a profit and loss statement and you are not an experienced chief financial officer (CFO), the numbers may make no sense. With some assistance, though, anyone can understand the basics. But what about the context? This is where things get tricky.

If everyone gets access to overviews of costs, incomes and profits, what might they do with that knowledge? In the first months of back-to-back profits, would employees all be asking for a pay rise? After several months of losses and bad news, would they all look for new jobs? These are tough questions with answers specific to your business. It may not be prudent for some companies to share the full information to those at the entry level, for a myriad of reasons. Maybe in a small business, it would be too easy to learn everyone's salary. This is something that does not fall under the umbrella of transparency and should always remain confidential. Or maybe certain financial elements cannot be released for strategic reasons. You will have to make the call on what is right for your situation. To make it easier, I'll let you know where to start, and what worked for my company.

The obvious starting point is with senior management. Everyone with a 'C' at the start of their title (CEO, CFO, chiefs of HR and information technology, etc) should have access to this information and be included in regular efforts to monitor and improve the company's bottom line. Next, take financial transparency down a level. Depending on the size of your company, those invited to share this information could be senior vice presidents, directors, managers or key staff. If you can, share the same information with them, or at least the numbers related to their area of influence. Get comfortable there, and again move it down the line.

Keep repeating this process as far as you can within the constraints of your situation. Now, a greater percentage (or all) of your staff are on the same page and can understand much more about your company's performance in the marketplace. What you will find, as the months progress, are better questions, better ideas and a highly connected workforce focused on your bottom line.

During the transition, it is best to present new financial information in person, at departmental meetings or talks broken down into smaller groups. For the uninitiated, you can provide supporting guidance, such as annotated sample spreadsheets, video tutorials or online group training.

We used a combination of these techniques at PeopleG2. Getting financial information out there relieved so much pressure on the responsible parties, who now had help coming from all directions. Employees approached me with fantastic ideas on how we might save money. Others weighed in on how they thought we might increase income. Before, when they were kept in the dark, these things did not occur to them. Jack Stack was right: the more they knew, the more they could help the company.

This type of transparency can strengthen your business as it builds good workplace culture. If you cannot show the full financials to everyone, try using an abridged summary. Operating from a source of common information, especially in the economic realm, can pay infinite dividends.

Pillar I review

What is transparency?

Transparency in a business context involves the free exchange of relevant information and the context with which to understand it.

Why is transparency valuable to corporate culture?

Acting from shared information increases team cohesiveness, opportunities for leadership, insights based on critical inquiry, knowledge dissemination and employee retention – all of which have a positive effect on company performance.

How can company transparency be increased?

Ways to incorporate transparency include raising employee awareness of staff roles and goals, personal communication styles, the acceptance of all viewpoints and company financial information.

Notes

1 Merriam-Webster (2017) [accessed 23 April 2017] Definition of transparent [Online] https://www.merriam-webster.com/dictionary/transparent; see also Businessdictionary.com (2017) [accessed 23 April 2017] Transparency [Online] http://www.businessdictionary.com/definition/transparency.html

2 Helm, B (2013) [accessed 18 July 2017] 5 Unexpected benefits of opening your books, *Inc.com* [Online] https://www.inc.com/burt-helm/five-benefits-of-opening-your-books.html

3 ibid.

4 Damasio, A (1994) *Descartes Error: Emotion, reason, and the human brain*, Penguin

5 ibid.

6 Dweck, C (2006) *Mindset: The new psychology of success*, Random House, New York

7 DISC Profile (2017) [accessed 19 July 2017] DISC Overview [Online] https://www.discprofile.com/what-is-disc/overview/

8 Marquet D (2012) *Turn the Ship Around! A true story of turning followers into leaders*, Penguin

9 TalentTalk, David Marquet (2015) [accessed 23 April 2017] [Online] http://www.talenttalkradio.com/e/david-marquet-01062015/

Pillar II: positivity

We like to think that the business world is focused positively – on growth, innovation and success. But, more realistically, day-to-day transactions often require ongoing problem solving and disaster control. This *what's on fire today?* stance trickles into company culture and can infuse it with an undercurrent of negativity or, at the very least, wariness. Suppose we were to flip the daily equation to instead one of *what's right?* Could we progress further and more quickly? You bet.

Positive energy is contagious. So is the other kind. My experience and research has shown me that positive energy far outgrows the negative, and has a considerably bigger impact on organizations. It is also reserved for those who practise and work at making it truly consistent and effective. In order to set the tone we want for our environment and culture, we must make a conscious effort to lend forward momentum more weight in our organizations than we do setbacks. It is great to be gung-ho on untangling snarls, but emphasizing problems holds us back from stepping out in new directions. We might hesitate to implement new policies because – *gasp!* – trouble could arise.

In a world where missteps can mean business collapse, one measure to counteract this natural tendency is to put improvement and innovation among our top concerns. Codify these as company goals in your mission and values statements. Write them on placards and post them alongside cultural objectives, like TRANSPARENCY, in your hallways and meeting rooms. When you are looking ahead to improvement, you are less likely to get mired in current sticking points or past failures. Yes, you will want to solve problems – so you can move on to bigger things, not sit and wait for the next shoe to drop.

A proven way to infuse difficult situations with positivity is to operate from a standpoint of what *is* working and make decisions from there, rather than labelling problems and wondering what to do about them. We will look at two working methodologies that experts have been using for decades: appreciative inquiry and positive deviance. Appreciative inquiry is defined as 'a philosophy and a methodology for positive change. It is founded on the simple assumption that human systems – teams, organizations and people – move in the direction of what they study, what they focus upon and what they talk about with regularity.'[1] Appreciative inquiry changes the way in which we frame challenges to make overcoming them more likely. Positive deviance is defined as 'based on the observation that in every community there are certain individuals or groups whose uncommon behaviours and strategies enable them to find better solutions to problems than their peers, while having access to the same resources and facing similar or worse challenges.[2] Positive deviance creates novel ways of approaching obviously compromised situations, like poverty and illness – or in a business context, perhaps, looming bankruptcy – with new avenues for change.

Besides looking for silver linings in what we do, we will touch on mental outlooks. How we speak also affects the office atmosphere, and company culture in general. Have you noticed how, in the dead of winter, when the sun comes out and the weather is mild, people frequently remark on this obvious fact? Their cheer is infectious, because almost everyone can agree that a sunny respite feels good.

Now, have you ever been caught in a clique that is given to gossip? Criticism and denigration develop into a running thread with these people. Get two of them together – especially if another is absent – and they will ferociously go on about what is wrong with the target of the day. If you want to be included in the group, you have to dive into this mess. If not, you will probably become their next victim.

Positivity, our next pillar of success, is a pre-emptive strike against the darkness that is bound to come with any business. When you start out on a good note, the tough times are easier to handle. If you focus on problems, instead, misfortune can take company morale and business performance down the drain with it. Let's start this chapter by pointing out the sunny side of the challenges that your company faces. Then, we will talk about how to incorporate that constructive atmosphere into your company culture.

Positive 'problem' solving

It is great to have role models – people who earn your respect and trust, and lead by example. Their knowledge and experience help you avoid pitfalls and embrace effective solutions. These, coincidentally, are the goals of appreciative inquiry, our first method for taking the 'problem' out of problem solving.

This is where my good friend Tenny Poole comes in. Tenny is a principal of several consultancies, including the Corporation for Positive Change and West Coast Center for Positive Change, which help companies implement appreciative inquiry practices. She came to this calling during a decade as vice president of HR for Experian, known best for its credit-reporting services. After struggling with traditional approaches to change, she and a number of her Experian peers learnt about appreciative inquiry and received training. She continued to utilize this new positive-change approach with extraordinary results. She later left Experian to spread the word with other companies.

I was fortunate to meet Tenny over a business lunch one day, during which our different styles of expressing our ideas on managing staff quickly became obvious. My language was a hodgepodge of theoretical terms and popular buzzwords. But I noticed that Tenny spoke more concisely, from a distinct lexicon that, I soon found out, came from her work in appreciative inquiry. This method for effecting change was initially developed in the 1980s by David Cooperrider and Suresh Srivastva, two researchers at Case Western Reserve University's Department of Organizational Behaviour.

The concept holds that group systems tend to advance in the direction set by their main areas of focus, study and discussion. For instance, if they concentrate on struggles, they will struggle. If they concentrate on achievement, they will achieve. This is a simplistic description, but it is echoed by today's popular 'power of positive thinking' and 'law of attraction' theories.

I listened to Tenny talk, and her ideas dovetailed nicely with my favourite business topic. Fascinated by the implications that this forward-thinking ideology could have on company culture, I took every opportunity to learn more from her. Then, I passed that information along to other entrepreneurs on an August 2016 edition of my radio show TalentTalk.[3] Now it is your turn to find out how this practice can instil positivity into your business environment and objectives.

Tenets of appreciative inquiry

When issues arise that need action, your outlook greatly influences the outcomes. Setting out to solve problems may seem positive and proactive, but on a contextual basis, it's not. The term *problem*, alone, is akin to words like *bleak* and *depressing*. Just hearing them brings you down. In order to find openings for improving a situation, we need to focus on what is working and build outward, essentially eliminating problems with positive acts.

This is the driving force behind appreciative inquiry. Rather than create a battlefield for attacking difficulties, it sets the stage for success. The Corporation for Positive Change describes this interactive, four-pronged approach like this:

The 4-D cycle

1 Discovery: identify and appreciate what works.

2 Dream: imagine what might be.

3 Design: develop systems and structures, leveraging the best of what was and what might be.

4 Destiny: implement or deliver the proposed design.[4]

This process can be used in any circumstance, to explore any topic, or to take advantage of any opportunity within your company. In the great cultures that I studied, none of the companies listed the 4-D process as its model for success. But each did incorporate some, or all four, of these tenets into its operating procedures. Like Tenny, in her days at Experian – and like me, in my fledgling stage of thinking on the subject – companies like Google and Apple integrated appreciative inquiry in their own ways, and they were and still are perceived, both internally and in public, as positive organizations. Figure 4.1 shows how building on core strengths reinforces the 4-D process, and vice versa.

Figure 4.1 Appreciative inquiry 4-D process

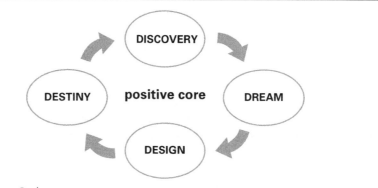

SOURCE Tenny Poole

Let's talk about the 4-D cycle in practical terms, using my company's experience as an example. As I mentioned in Chapter 3, as a way to avoid developing a fixed mindset about our clients, PeopleG2 began to survey every customer that had placed an order that month. To reflect their customer experience, users followed an online link to choose from one of three 'moods' depicted by drawings of faces: one was happy, one was neutral and one was sad. A simple click gave us a great data point to understand how we were doing in satisfying their needs. Based on their initial responses, a prompt for an optional second question would appear. If clients were happy, we asked them to tell us why – what went well, and who specifically might have done a great job for them. If they chose the neutral or sad face, we asked them to explain why they felt that way and to list any specifics that would help us understand their complaint.

For the first year, in 2015, we compiled happy-face ratings in the 99 per cent range. The rare neutral face would come in, and we dealt with it. But in early 2016, after some tremendous growth, we noticed a drop in customer satisfaction. Responses were still good, hovering around 90 per cent happy, but now approximately 10 per cent were not. This was a troubling trend. We did not want to sacrifice quality and satisfaction for growth.

In the past, before Tenny introduced me to the wonders of appreciative inquiry, we might have tried to figure out how to stamp out one problem at a time. Instead, we used the 4-D process to revamp our customer service model, going forward. Here's how we did it.

Discovery

Our customer service team started with *discovery* to find and evaluate what was working. Clearly, the survey was. It was giving us measurable feedback on a regular basis, in a more objective manner than our previous interpretations of random talks with clients. By contacting clients and questioning them, rather than waiting for them to call us, we increased our opportunities to get information that we would have otherwise missed. To learn more, we looked for patterns in that information.

The nature of the optional comments showed that the survey format freed clients to bring up specifics, making them more likely to give us honest answers over time. It may seem strange, but not everyone enjoys complaining. Many people prefer to avoid a conflict or difficult conversation. In the past, when dissatisfied customers had to take the initiative to express their displeasure, they might simply take their business elsewhere, and we would lose them as a client and never find out why. But, sending our survey out every month demonstrated our desire to know the truth. Its simplicity and the option for open-ended comment conveyed respect for our customers' time and feedback.

After the fixed-mindset incident, we realized that we had to build trust with our clients and show that we valued their opinions, good and bad. Most importantly, we had to open up communication channels in which they felt it was okay to give us bad news. What we learned in our discovery phase was that developing greater trust enabled clients to give us detailed and forthright answers.

This first 'D' in the cycle allows people to savour the good that they find. Our team also took the time to appreciate the human process that was working. They recognized the value of staff members who not only identified complaints and compliments, but acted on them to help customers.

Dream

The team then moved on to *dream*, to envision our immediate goal for customer satisfaction. This 'D' proved to be uncomfortable for the team. What would they dream for this process, in a perfect world? Was it 100 per cent client satisfaction? We wondered if such an ideal was even an appropriate wish.

The team wrestled with this over the course of several meetings. They eventually came up with two distinct ideas for the wish list. The first was for the company to work towards and believe it could achieve 100 per cent happy-face customer satisfaction ratings each month. The second idea had to do with transparency, and showed how this line of inquiry prompted more creative thinking. What if we worried less about the 100 per cent mark, and more about a process?

We felt as though we had hit on something. This positive approach said: instead of trying to be perfect, why don't we simply accept that sometimes things will not be perfect? Sometimes clients will complain. Sometimes they will have things to complain about. In this case, *how we responded* and worked with the client were more important than chasing a good record. Then what?

Extrapolating from what we had discovered was working well, we felt it would be beneficial to enhance the environment that made it safe for clients to share their honest opinions. Then we could do our best to help. When we saw what worked there, we could make incremental changes each month. Another positive step would be sharing our results with clients and our entire staff.

It was easy to see that creating opportunities to help clients instead of just to solve problems was the best road to take. This fundamental shift has been instrumental to my company's subsequent success. The power of this second 'D' lay in the team members going through this *dream* process and enjoying the space to think about how the future might look. The opportunity to think and explore different ideas and approaches was vital to their ultimate decision.

Design

Having dreamed about what we wanted to happen, it was time to devise a means of effecting that outcome. We put the momentum gained from the first two phases to work for the *design* part of the cycle. Fortunately, we already had the bones of a functioning system in place. The survey process was getting results, and we had ideas for how to improve on that tool. We had discovered that it became more effective over time, as clients grew comfortable with using it each month. And we had plans to close the feedback loop by e-mailing clients and account representatives periodically about the outcomes. That sounded good to me. But, the team said they wanted to go deeper.

I'm always open to ideas, even if I think I've got the right ones, and the turn that this third 'D' took shows why diversity in thinking is valuable. I would be shocked and pleased by the team's findings.

Having a variety of measurement tools paid off for us. In searching for underlying patterns in how effective our customer service was, we realized that certain people were more effective than others in handling complaints, delivering solutions and allowing clients to feel safe in sharing bad news. Cross-referencing with DISC personality reports showed that these individuals tended to be introverts. Their communication styles were perceived as less threatening, making them far more effective in identifying, responding to and resolving customer concerns. The consensus reached was that the customer service team should be designed, as best we could, to include more introverts.

As a card-carrying extrovert, I was sceptical. So, our 'designers' shared with me 120 customer communications received in the previous year that contained complaints or other bad news about our performance – and the final outcomes, broken down by employee. The introverts were running circles around us extroverts! Customers served by introverts showed higher satisfaction in issue resolution. Among those employees, client retention was almost 100 per cent, and they were getting better data for making improvements than those with more outgoing natures.

Now, does that mean you should only hire introverts to perform customer service? I am not ready to make that recommendation across the board. We work with a lot of HR professionals, and at least half of them could be classified as extroverts. I don't know what their ratings look like. For us, though, a very specific design – based on information that we had gathered – promised to enable us to work more effectively and make our clients happier.

Destiny

To their credit, the team did not want these revelations to be forgotten in a few months or a year. They wanted their design to stick. So, when we talked about *destiny*, they were excited to be entering the implementation phase. In it, we put machinery in place to encourage perpetual motion on the issue.

Now, once a month, the customer service team presents their survey findings and a summary of opportunities to help clients at our all-staff meeting. As designed, they are sharing ideas and outcomes internally and allowing for more improvements outside their department. There have been times when someone in Sales, Information Technology (IT) or Marketing hears something in a summary that inspires them. They feel welcome to bring complementary ideas, system tweaks and more to the table. This open process helped us develop an ideal model for hiring in other areas of the company. Analysing our most effective people against their DISC profiles, we created an ideal set of characteristics to look for as we add to or replace members on the team.

Rating the 4-D cycle

We found the interdependent nature of the four 'D' tenets invigorating and effective. Each stage builds on the last, and each stage supports our company's core strengths. That is a far cry from just focusing on problems. But because nothing goes smoothly for ever, we realized that this process must be continual. Our team agreed to revisit it annually, to respond to whichever challenges or opportunities for improvement arise. By doing so, the tasks would become more manageable over time.

This incident showed us that appreciative inquiry could positively affect many of our operations. Imagine using the four 'Ds' yourself to develop better meetings, improve sales, lower costs and foster an overall better company culture. The options are limitless for companies that value and practise positivity.

Our customer service dilemma, however, was not exactly life and death. It may have foretold a worse decline, had we not addressed it, but the company probably would have survived in our old problem-solving mode. What happens when you face a real crisis? Yes, appreciative inquiry principles will help. You can add to your toolbox, however, another positive technique that Tenny Poole told me about, positive deviance – one that literally did save lives.

Applying positive deviance

Recall that positive deviance is an unorthodox way of bringing about change from within a compromised situation. In this context, the people with the solutions are not outside experts with ready resources, but those affected by the difficulty who find a new way of approaching it. You will find the details in the book *The Power of Positive Deviance: How unlikely innovators solve the world's toughest problems*, by Richard Pascale, Jerry Sternin and Monique Sternin.[5] In illuminating the role of positive deviance, the authors recount the kind of feel-good story that Hollywood might one day immortalize in film. The story that Tenny used to pique my interest involved malnourished children who were living in abject poverty in Vietnam. Attempts by humanitarians to ease their woes had failed time and again – until the light bulb went on for someone who lived in those conditions day to day.

In 1990, the Vietnamese government requested relief assistance from the international nongovernmental organization (NGO) Save the Children. The NGO tapped Jerry Sternin, an American staff member who had been doing similar work in the Philippines, to go to Vietnam and assess and address the plight of malnourished and starving children. Sternin and his wife, Monique, and young son, Sam, accepted the challenge and moved to Hanoi.

At that time, the US government was still enforcing an embargo on Vietnam, and the ghosts of the Vietnam War were far from gone. The Sternins were among fewer than two dozen Americans to reside in that city as of 1990. Given the circumstances, Sternin was allowed a six-month window to do what might take years. He and the team he brought in would have to prove they could help, or get out. Their job was to alleviate child malnutrition, but a larger problem awaited them. The locals didn't want them there.

Residents had already been disillusioned by past failed efforts. In the village targeted for aid, more than half of the children still faced starvation. The government would come in with supplies and help, the kids would start to get better, but then supply chains would break down or funding would fall short. Children were dying. If Sternin could develop a programme showing short-term results, his team might be allowed to stay longer, perhaps thwarting a major epidemic and saving tens of thousands of lives.

Sternin's team began gathering baseline information about the children's physical environment in the village, and what, when and how much they ate. Amid suspicion and distrust, they managed to secure family information such as who cared for the children and other data points. Sternin admits that near the end of this process, everything seemed bleak: 64 per cent of the village children were undernourished and at risk of starvation. The team felt less than confident about learning anything new that would help them fulfil their mission.

Here is where it gets interesting. If 64 per cent of children are starving, what do you ask next? Most people jump to the problem: the 64 per cent. Why are they malnourished? Is it poverty? Lack of food? Too many children in the family? Poor government intervention? At this point, Sternin remembered reading about the concept of positive deviance. Similar to appreciative inquiry, this theory employs 'somersault questions' to flip the focus from what is not functioning to what is. Instead of asking why the 64 per cent are starving, Sternin thought, shouldn't we ask why the other 36 per cent are *not* malnourished?

The team did. The common assumption was that the kids who were well fed came from families above the poverty line. So, Sternin's questions needed to break through assumptions. Were there any well-fed children from very poor families? The surprising answer – which exemplifies the power of positive deviance – was yes. It was possible for a child from a poverty-stricken family to be well nourished.

Those who were had a few things in common. First, each morning someone from the family went out to the rice paddy and found small shrimp or crabs and certain wild plants to add to the children's rice. Second, because smaller children process smaller portions, their parents or care givers fed them small meals, four or five times a day. Other malnourished children were eating only twice a day. Third, the children's hands were washed at every meal, and again if the child came into contact with anything unclean. This likely limited the spread of disease, a factor that affects proper digestion and weight retention.

What Sternin and his team discovered was a solution that many local families had already embraced. Once they did that, the government was able to change its approach and make truly life-saving contributions.

Holy smokes. When I read that, my head almost spun around. The solution had been there all along; it was people's assumptions and mindsets that prevented them from seeing it.

Immediately, applications for this way of thinking started to flood my mind. I would be able to answer questions that were important to the future of PeopleG2: *Why do people like to work for my company? Why do my customers stay with us? What are my best salespeople doing? What do we do well?* The list went on and on. Focusing on the things that were going right was like shining a beacon of light on a ship navigating stormy seas at night.

Putting positivity into practice

In addition to using appreciative and deviant modes of inquiry to address challenges, what we say during the process can affect the outcome. Allowing employees to reflect on what is working can prompt changes in the tone of day-to-day conversations. Remember how just hearing the word *depressing* is depressing? A similar dynamic is at work when we adopt positive speech patterns. Research shows that our linguistic context is also important to maintaining a constructive outlook.

A 2015 study published in the *Journal of Applied Psychology* showed us that positive and optimistic interactions elevated team effectiveness. Researchers reviewed 39 independent studies of 2,799 groups. They found that 'group positive affect (or, in lay terms, optimism) has consistent positive effects on social integration and task performance',[6] unrelated to any other factors. Period. The influence of negativity depended on what else was going on at the time. My translation: positivity works. People and groups do well when we use encouraging words and contexts that are positive. Here are two great ways to practise doing that.

Just say 'yes'

Imagine what might happen if you said yes to everything. Not just to those questions you like or want to be asked. What would happen if you chose to say yes all the time? Would your life change?

Before you conclude that this is not possible, I'll tell you a secret. I have been saying yes to everything, when possible, since 2014. This simple switch has opened doors that changed my life and perspective for ever. It is also the easiest way to start practising positivity.

Your first reaction to this pronouncement was probably scepticism. *What if all my employees asked for a raise? What if my spouse gives me a list of chores when I really want to do something else on the weekend?* Never mind the ways in which this is not feasible. Let's think of a mundane context in which we do have the option of agreeing, instead of disagreeing.

This trick is used in comedy improvisation. Actors working on extemporaneous comedy are instructed to start talking, and say 'yes, and' or 'yes, but' to each question or statement – often with hilarious results. It keeps a dialogue going that surprises the audience with counterintuitive turns. We expect, in a line of questioning, that answers will be split between yes and no. But a *no* answer could effectively end the improvised dialogue, so we hear an incongruous *yes*.

We don't all have to be comedians to practise this trick. Let's look at the different attitudes expressed in a typical exchange and a 'say yes' exchange. Here I am talking to a fictional friend at a hypothetical birthday party:

Sally: Chris, would you like some ice cream?

Chris: Maybe; depends on what flavour you have.

Sally: How about mint chocolate chip?

Chris: I don't like that kind. Do you have strawberry?

Sally: Sure. Is one scoop enough?

Chris: No. Give me two.

It was subtle, but some negativity came through here. First, I didn't really acknowledge Sally, although she called me by name. Beyond that, indicating that I don't like mint chocolate chip ice cream was really not needed. I may have annoyed Sally by disparaging what she had to offer, and then I didn't acquiesce to what she did offer, but demanded more. Suppose I had been in 'yes' mode, instead:

Sally: Chris, would you like some ice cream?

Chris: Yes, and I would love two scoops.

Sally: Sure; how about mint chocolate chip?

Chris: Yes, thank you, Sally. But, if you have it, I would prefer strawberry flavour.

Sally: Of course.

Here, I could eat my favourite ice cream, say yes to Sally, and not leave her with anything negative. But this was a generalization. Now, let's apply this technique to a more difficult business conversation. Pretend that you are the manager in this scenario:

Bob: Can I have a pay rise?

Manager: No.

Bob: But, I work really hard.

Manager: We only consider pay rises during the annual review process.

Bob: It's a long time until my annual review. Would you think about giving me a pay rise now, instead?

You: No.

Having a set policy that only allows for one outcome, in this case, speaks for itself. At least for most of the year, that conversation is going to be negative. Next, let's find some positivity in the situation:

Bob: Can I have a pay rise?

Manager: That's possible, yes.

Bob: Really? Okay. How soon will that take effect?

Manager: Well, we can take the first step. Let's review your departmental goals and your track record to date. Then we can check in on a regular basis to ensure you are on track for your annual review. That's when we make salary decisions.

Bob: So, if I meet my goals, I'll get a pay rise around the time of my annual review?

You: Yes.

Of course, the company may not be on solid footing at that time, or might have to allocate funds for another purpose. But, at the time that Bob asked you, your positive statements were true. By saying yes whenever possible, we inject hope, possibility and positivity into the conversation. As the boss, agreeing to consider Bob's request removes you as the blocker, or the person telling him no. Instead of making a black-and-white judgement call, you redirected the conversation to give Bob some control over the situation as you conformed with company policy. Now the pay rise hinges on his ability or his success in meeting the agreed-upon goals.

This technique is so powerful. In fact, just reading it might not give you the full understanding of how effective this trick can be in daily life, perhaps because you don't realize that the opposite tendency is stifling your good nature. Screenwriter Shonda Rhimes points out this dichotomy in her best-selling book, *Year of Yes: How to dance it out, stand in the sun and be your own person*.[7] She relates that, despite her professional success in Hollywood, she had a reputation among friends and family for saying no to social engagements. One day, she mentioned that she had received some interesting invitations to visit famous people in exotic places. Her sister Delores dismissed the subject. 'Who cares?' Delores said. 'You're just going to say "no" anyway.'

This was the wake-up call Rhimes needed. She knew that her excuses had closed her off from many of life's opportunities. She resolved to say yes to everything for a year, a satisfying journey that she describes in her book. So, if an introverted workaholic known for saying no can switch to yes, you can as well.

The obstacle to overcome is to make a conscious choice to do it. Saying yes – which sounds easy – is hard to do when your brain is on autopilot and you act out of habit. To make a change, start off in small chunks. Maybe you do *yes* on Monday. Or how about *yes* to just your friends or family first? Pick a focus and give it a try. Once you have formed a new habit, you will naturally use this technique at work. Just remember the comedian's trick – 'yes, and' or 'yes, but' – and everyone from employees to teenagers will respond more positively.

Give 'feedforward' not feedback

What happens to our language when we are faced with something other than yes or no questions? According to a 2015 collaborative study published in *Group & Organization Management*, positive talk promotes positive action – and vice versa. US and European researchers found that, like the principles at play in appreciative inquiry and positive deviance, constructive comments beget similar actions. At the same time, problem-focused language and efforts lead to more of the same.

After analysing more than 43,000 utterances made by over 40 problem-solving teams in two organizations, these psychologists had some simple advice for executives: 'Managers should develop an awareness of how the moment-to-moment conversational dynamics in team interactions contribute to positivity spirals and ultimately to team performance.'[8] So, not only does pep talk work in the short term, it causes a *spiral* of positive thoughts and actions.

You can see for yourself how this works in business dynamics by testing out a sample exercise devised by Marshall Goldsmith. A prolific author and editor, his works include two *New York Times* bestsellers, a *Wall Street Journal* number-one business book, and a Harold Longman Business Book of the Year. Marshall Goldsmith is such a highly decorated thinker in the fields of business and education that, when he agreed to be a guest on my radio show, I devoted the entire hour to talking with him on TalentTalk.[9] During his interview, he mentioned a new term I had never heard before: *feedforward*, which is obviously the antithesis of feedback. The latter involves commentary through hindsight. The former is a future-facing means of providing input that is inherently more positive than the alternative.

Goldsmith describes why this process works in more detail in a 2014 article he wrote for *Inc.* magazine: 'We can change the future. We cannot change the past. Feedforward helps people envision and focus on a positive future, not a failed past. By giving people ideas on how they can be even more successful (as opposed to visualizing a failed past), we can increase their chances of achieving this success in the future.'[10] Sounds like common sense, doesn't it? Yet managers persist in delivering their considered opinions once it is too late – as feedback.

You can try Goldsmith's exercise using real-life issues at your next meeting. To do so, ask your team to pair off, and have each person tell their partner what they need from them going forward. That's it. When they finish, their partner does the same for them. Then, everyone changes partners until each person has shared with at least three other people, including the one in charge of the meeting. The results? New ideas for what is to come, and a positivity spiral arising from the ways in which you discussed it.

Part of the reason for this is that you have removed the negative blockers *and* you have removed the possibility of blame from the equation. With feedback, the giver is usually analysing what the receiver did in the past. As Goldsmith points out in the *Inc.* article, people do not always take this type of criticism well. Feedforward, on the other hand, he says, 'cannot involve a personal critique, since it is discussing something that has not yet happened'!

We discovered this benefit first hand at PeopleG2. The concept of feedback now feels so negative to us – and we recognize when others employ feedforward effectively. I was sitting in a meeting at another office once, when a manager announced, 'Hey everyone! I need you to shut off your computers and pay attention to me this time. Also, John, could you let other people talk once in a while? Great. Thanks!' I laughed out loud by accident, and everyone asked what was so funny. I told them about feedforward, and heads started nodding. After asking a few questions, it was apparent that John's behaviour had been going on for weeks and nothing had worked to change it. I predicted that it probably would now.

Pillar II review

Where does positivity fit into company culture?

Positive thoughts, words and actions have been shown to elevate work performance.

How do conventional problem-solving models fall short?

Problem-focused thoughts, words and actions have the opposite effect of positive ones. They create a fixed mindset and make circumventing obstacles more difficult.

How does positivity affect problem solving?

Positivity in exploring solutions helps people focus on what works well, and then build on that to eliminate what is causing problems.

Notes

1 Corporation for Positive Change (2015) [accessed 16 October 2017] Appreciative inquiry (AI [Online] https://positivechange.org/how-we-work/appreciative-inquiry-ai/

2 Positive Deviance Initiative (2016) [accessed 21 July 2017] What Is Positive Deviance [Online] http://www.positivedeviance.org/

3 TalentTalk, Matt Perry and Tenny Poole (2016) [accessed 21 July 2017] [Online] http://www.talenttalkradio.com/e/matt-perry-and-tenny-poole-08092016/

4 Corporation for Positive Change (2015) [accessed 21 July 2017] How the 4-D process works [Online] https://positivechange.org/how-the-4-d-process-works/

5 Pascale, R, Sternin, J and Sternin, M (2010) *The Power of Positive Deviance: How unlikely innovators solve the world's toughest problems*, Harvard Business School Publishing, Boston, MA

6 Knight, A P and Eisenkraft, N (2015) [accessed 6 May 2017] Positive is usually good, negative is not always bad: The effects of group affect on social integration and task performance, *Journal of Applied Psychology* [Online] https://www.ncbi.nlm.nih.gov/pubmed/25495091?dopt=Abstract

7 Rhimes, S (2015) *Year of Yes: How to dance it out, stand in the sun and be your own person*, Simon & Schuster, New York

8 Lehmann-Willenbrock, N, Chiu, M M, Lei, Z and Kauffeld, S (2016) [accessed 21 July 2017] Understanding positivity within dynamic team interactions: A statistical discourse analysis, *Group & Organization Management* [Online] http://journals.sagepub.com/doi/full/10.1177/1059601116628720

9 TalentTalk (2015) [accessed 6 May 2017] Marshall Goldsmith [Online] http://www.talenttalkradio.com/e/marshall-goldsmith-08052014/

10 Goldsmith, M (2014) [accessed 6 May 2017] Instead of feedback, try feedforward to boost team performance, Inc.com [Online] https://www.inc.com/marshall-goldsmith/power-of-feedforward.html

Pillar III: measurement

Measurement counterbalances our human inclination to make sense of things we don't understand. Given a set of facts, we try to make sense of them, by applying our experiences and what we have learnt in order to fill in the gaps. Sometimes we are right, but very often we are wrong. You will recall from our discussion about the jerboa in Chapter 3 that we call that glitch a cognitive bias.

When our powers of mental judgement fail us, however, measuring data can save the day. One of many cognitive biases that can trip us up is our tendency to cast greater importance on recent events than those that occurred further in the past. We are likely to use this temporal yardstick when making decisions, even if more objective measures would be more effective. For example, if a terrorist just blew up an airplane, we worry about it happening again as it is fresh in our minds, not to mention memorable. We might postpone travel plans for that reason, whereas only probability calculations from long-term data trends could tell us if our risk has really increased.

Let's move this bias into the workplace. If you have a salesperson who brought in a big, new account, does that prove they are a top performer? You might think so, if it happened just before an annual review and you are wondering how to rate that person. If you look over relevant spreadsheets, though, you might conclude that this salesperson missed their goals, failed to reach quota for the year, and consistently underperformed. The numbers tell you to overlook the timely account win and make a better decision about that salesperson.

When it comes to business performance, the numbers tell the truth, and valuing this combination – numbers and truth – is a hallmark of great company culture. As Laszlo Bock said about Google, 'we measure everything'. This meant everything from computer code quality to how much money was spent on executive travel.[1] Placing great stock in the analysis of such figures allows companies to use those findings to their advantage. These days, the more extensive the findings, the bigger the advantage.

Because Google's operation is so huge, so are its data sets. Researchers are using this type of 'big data' to revolutionize planning, public policy and technologies with insights that were not possible before computers could handle so much volume. Information gained by discovering highly significant trends and correlations can have predictive and preventive benefits. For instance, IBM's Watson, a computerized question-answering system, holds immense potential for medical solutions.[2] It analyses enormous amounts of source data and generates hypotheses that help doctors diagnose more accurately, search for better cures and prevent disease.

Besides large-scale applications like Watson's, computer technology is bringing big-data measurement to us on a personal level. Our smartphone apps already collect and dispense data – think tracking your shopping preferences and giving you GPS directions to the store. Consumer products like wireless activity trackers and smartwatches have begun tallying our movement, respiration, heart rate, etc – all for the purpose of learning more about them, and more about the systems of which they are a part.

What do all of these instruments have in common? Measurement. In this chapter, we will talk about: what the numbers can do for your company's culture and performance; what is important to measure and analyse (and what is not); how to gather information; and what do to with that knowledge.

The value of measurement and big data

How can CEOs and HR managers use big-data concepts to improve operations? Suppose we had a gadget to assess employee engagement, happiness and productivity. The science for this is well under way, and you might already own one of these by the time you buy this book. If so, you will be well positioned to raise this next pillar of success. Because, among the companies I studied, those with the best cultures are leading the way and implementing the results of big-data measurement wherever they can. This brings us back to Google.

An outfit with healthy culture has no problem taking a hard look at its practices. So those at Google wondered why some teams were consistently successful, while others were not as effective. Julia Rozovsky, manager of People Analytics, tells the story of how the company used deep data analysis to find out. Over two years they studied about 180 teams, conducting 200 interviews and looking at 250 personality traits. They expected that some magic combination of extroverts and introverts, or management with technical expertise, or some other formula would surface. In fact, team effectiveness had nothing to do with individual personality traits. It hinged on the ability to interact in an effective manner, which in turn hinged on other factors.

In interpreting the results of this examination, they found that the more effective teams usually could say yes to these five questions:

---

1 **Psychological safety:** can we take risks on this team without feeling insecure or embarrassed?

2 **Dependability:** can we count on each other to do high-quality work on time?

3 **Structure and clarity:** are goals, roles and execution plans on our team clear?

4 **Meaning of work:** are we working on something that is personally important for each of us?

5 **Impact of work:** do we fundamentally believe that the work we are doing matters?[3]

The beauty of measuring trends and getting results is that those results can then be analysed for further connections. The Google number crunchers learned that not only were those five factors important, the first and foremost element to team cohesion was psychological safety. With it, the other goals could be achieved. Without it, basically there was no team.

In fact, the company found that just talking over these needs when teams were formed made them likely to be highly effective. This measurable outcome led to more data analysis, and the creation of policies and exercises to capitalize on the knowledge, which led to – you guessed it – more ways to measure group improvement.

When performance measurement leads to better performance and more strategic ways to measure it, we find another kind of positivity spiral that propels the company forward. One that puts powerful analytics into action. There is now so much data, however, that the real trick is to know where to focus, and what to measure, to achieve your best results.

What to measure and why

So, what should you start 'counting' in your organization? For our purposes, anything that plays into your company's culture and market success is fair game. It could be people, budget figures, project objectives or integrations. Once you understand the driving forces and trends involved in their activity, you can better manage their outcomes.

But, before you get started compiling data, prioritize what you wish to learn. Is it the reason behind a downturn? Or a chance to capitalize on a strength? Having a tight focus will make your strategy pay off. Here is how to determine the most important place to start.

Key performance indicators

This is no time to play favourites, looking for numbers that support what you *wish* would happen. Take a step back and work with your team members to determine which unifying events occur just before you hit a marker of success or failure. These are called **key performance indicators** (KPIs). They might be noticeable customer attrition, new sales, delinquent accounts, product defects or increased profits. In other words, if profits go up, you are about to succeed in meeting a goal. If a product defect comes to light and goes public, you may be about to fail, financially and in terms of company image.

Looking at flags that can help you predict good or bad fortune or performance will help you decide exactly what to measure and analyse. Since KPIs can tip you off in advance, your organization will have a chance to change course – or if you discover performance correlations after the fact, you will know what to do next time. So, spend some time talking over your KPI thresholds and how measuring these criteria can help you prevent failure and leverage success.

For example, one area in which companies typically struggle is with onboarding new staff. A poor onboarding process costs time, talent and money. A more in-depth or efficient process pays off and saves those resources over time. You can use data analysis to see where your business stands on these issues. Here is one way to do it.

Suppose you noticed an increase in staff attrition in recent months. You might want to run the numbers on how many employees were lost, say, in a quarter, relative to the same time period in past years. You might also want to check on how long those people worked for your company in total. Long-term employees as a group might have different reasons for leaving than short-term employees. When turnover times decrease, though, it typically indicates an overlooked, underlying problem. If the HR data shows a significant percentage of people quitting soon after hire – say, within the first 90 days – your balance sheet is bleeding and you are facing greater losses than usual. Now would be the time to add this metric as a KPI.

When one of these indicators lights up, it is time to find out why, since the situation is likely to trigger something big. In the case of attrition, you might survey the employee, their co-workers and boss. Find out why these people are leaving. Then you can do something about it.

Quick exits may suggest that the employees in question felt unable to do the job they had accepted. It might be about their skill sets – they realize, too late, that they are not well equipped. But, more often, it is about the level of support they get as a new hire. Starting a new job is not easy, and not everyone is flexible enough to learn, understand and perform it on their own. You can look into how they did perform during their short tenure.

As you review the survey results, you may find that lost employees did not have the tools and access they needed to be successful. They may have had inadequate introductions to their team early on, no access to organizational charts, or scant time with their boss in which to learn not just job parameters, but the company's mission, values and vision. People tend to show up for their first day on the job energized and ready to go. Too often, they become frustrated when they show up, receive a packet of forms to fill out, and are plopped in front of a screen to watch a generic informational video. Then they eat lunch alone. After lunch, they are expected to figure out how to work and what to do, with no expressed goals, no direction and no help. I've seen it myself, and can infer from reviewing other companies' intake practices that it happens all the time!

Suppose you collect the hiring and attrition data and learn through surveys that a rough initial experience caused new hires to feel overwhelmed and lose confidence in their ability to contribute to the company. It follows that a better onboarding experience should reduce the incidence of hasty exits. With that in place, the drain on company resources in locating talent, onboarding them, losing them and starting over again will slow. Not having to pay for ads, recruiters, interviews and background checks means that financials will improve. So, if you could make the intake process better, everyone wins.

Incorporate this into your company's data analysis system. The number of staff retained or lost in the first quarter could be your KPI. You might discover your threshold of absorbing the new-hire cost to be one employee per 90 days – in other words, you can afford that much in turnover costs. So, you can set your goal at 9 out of 10 new hires remaining through their first three months. You would start adjusting your hiring process and measuring how each incremental change impacts your KPI. These steps might include:

- Giving the applicant the necessary documents to complete before their formal starting date.

- Assigning an onboarding partner to answer questions, take them to lunch on their first day, and liaison with team members.

- Having their business cards ready on day one.

- Getting their phone number, e-mail account and computer passwords set up and ready, day one.
- Discussing their goals, milestones and objectives for their first 90 days on day one.
- Planning meetings with their boss and team, day one.
- Providing a gift box of everything they might need for their first day such as pens, paper and contact lists – plus a welcome note from the CEO.
- Surveying them after their first day, week and month to measure job satisfaction.
- Meeting with HR on a regular basis to track progress and job fit.

Besides company-wide KPIs, HR professionals can measure employee-specific KPIs. What is it that your people do that is crucial to meeting their performance objectives? These may trigger the success or failure of that staff member, which in turn affects overall business fortunes. According to *Harvard Business Review*, one HR director, Bernard McGovern of LG Electronics USA, studies his employees' revenue, profitability or service KPIs three times a year. These help the company to set goals and reward achievement.[4]

Taking this approach with any type of KPI can help companies improve in the areas that have the most impact on the business. We will talk more about how to systematize your data collection and analysis in a moment. To determine effective KPIs, use the 'SMART goal' approach. This set of five criteria was devised in the 1980s and is commonly accepted today as a best practice. Ensure that any KPI you set is:

Specific: use specific, rather than open-ended goals; you should be able to clearly define them in one sentence.

Measurable: be sure the KPI can be objectively quantified – such as which resources were available to an employee versus how they felt.

Attainable: be confident you can get enough *actionable* data that, once implemented, can be further assessed.

Realistic: set only the KPI goals that meet the above criteria and whose results will significantly impact the company.

Time based: use time periods as a metric that will let you analyse the right amount of data and act appropriately.

Don't forget this last concept! Some data can look good in the short term, but be problematic long term – or, a trend that builds slowly or erratically might not become apparent in the short run. So, use all of these SMART boundaries to help you focus your research on the most important factors to either staff or company performance. Why? Because, as you set your KPIs and review the areas that will have the most impact on your business, you will start to see immediate results. This should lead to a commitment to continue collecting and using data, the way Google does.

A word of caution, though: from that excitement may come a tendency to want to measure *everything*. By measuring everything, we also start managing everything. Remember our early lessons in Chapter 2 about the foundations of good company culture. We do not want to start overmeasuring and micromanaging; this would strip away autonomy, stifle mastery and diminish our purpose. To be safe, remember to **measure to manage** at the right level, and to **measure to gain clarity**. Focus on those areas you know you should manage, and where greater clarity helps you to make better choices.

Now that you are on your way to generating measurable markers, let's talk about how to collect data on those all-important points.

How and where to get information

You will find two ways to gather information about your company – to compile past and real-time outcomes. The first type comes in the form of surveys and reports of things that have already occurred: customer satisfaction surveys, employee opinion surveys, performance reviews, company website analytics, and so on. Real-time work and progress can be measured as it happens, digitally and through self-analysis and third-party observation.

Compiling a large amount of data will give you the most insights. Innovation in this area has brought us many tools. In addition to supercomputers like IBM's Watson – which may be out of your price range – we have search-engine optimization (SEO) and analytics to track website performance; customer relationship management (CRM) systems such as Salesforce to rate sales and the customer experience; and online crowdsourced solutions such as Glassdoor to record employee satisfaction. You might institute periodic surveys, like PeopleG2 does with our monthly customer accounts. Speaking of periodic assessments, are you wondering when to measure? The answer to that is, *often*.

Measure frequently

Because collecting and measuring data keeps getting easier and the findings more sophisticated, companies should be moving towards frequency. Besides allowing companies to act quickly on impending business circumstances, frequent assessments requiring human input make it easier to provide honest information. Short-term recall is simply better. For instance, is it easier for you to remember what you had for dinner a year ago, or last night?

I once thought that, if I could, I would wave a magic wand and make annual employee reviews disappear for ever. I dislike their structure and all the problems they create. Here is how they usually work: once a year, a manager – who may or may not have been your boss for the previous 12 months – is charged with evaluating you. This manager must strain to remember all that you did – or did not do – in the past, or rely on second-hand information, if they are new to the post. In some instances, they are instructed to give you just enough praise to keep you going, but not enough that you demand a large pay rise.

In my world where magic wands exist, I would also remove the entire discussion of money from annual reviews. Remember the Harvard study I mentioned in Chapter 2, which found an inverse relationship, in certain situations, between cash bonuses and work performance? The annual review juncture is the worst time to stir this pot. It sets the tone for the next 12 months. So what's my suggestion? Forget the wand, and work the magic yourself.

At PeopleG2, we don't conduct annual reviews – we conduct *monthly* reviews. Each month, all employees rate themselves on about five goals, which are unique to each person and position. They also rate their performance on five competencies that we feel are important for the entire organization that month. Then, their managers do the same. The combined self-assessment and manager's evaluation result in a score and an explanatory report.

How you analyse staff is not as important as doing it often. Instead of one make-or-break review, each person has 12 interactions a year with their boss to check in on goals and skills that are fresh in both of their minds. You will notice that greater frequency also allows PeopleG2 to focus on goals that are particularly relevant that month.

More frequent assessment helps us to move forward more quickly too. As individuals complete goals, we can add new goals. There may be a larger, long-term objective in place, and this lets us move towards it steadily, month to month, while not becoming overwhelmed by its scope. Here, the focus is on the micro, not the macro, goals. But, we are using these micro events to ensure the macro mission is successfully achieved.

Measure at the right time

Frequency is not the only timing issue in data collection. *When* you ask a question can influence the answers you will get. Take employee surveys about how things are working within the company. Most organizations are still going through this ritual once a year, which is as problematic as it is with annual performance reviews. First, employees are being formally asked just once a year for their opinions on company operations. When does this happen? The timing could skew the results.

If you ask when business is slower, such as in December, you might get a different answer than you would when things are busy. Asking financial questions at different times might render different answers – for example, at the beginning of springtime versus 15 April, when US employees file their tax returns.

A second issue around the timing of surveys is when the results will prompt action. Suppose that the data you have collected in your annual survey is useful. Now management needs to review the information and decide what to do next. This could take months of meetings, preparation and planning. It's possible that, from the time you start working at a firm in January and then take a survey in December, management might have no opportunity to respond or act on the results until the following June. This means that 18 months can pass in which some easily addressed problems are left untouched, or a new-found strength ignored.

Despite our best intentions, issues often do not percolate to the top. That situation is a nightmare for employees. To counter this at PeopleG2, we instituted a weekly survey of a single question, to which users may respond anonymously. By doing this weekly, I get 52 questions answered per year, and I can respond and set the pace of change accordingly. We prefer questions that are open-ended and draw out answers that go beyond yes or no. With just one question before them, employees can take the time to think more deeply about a topic than if it were buried among dozens more. This delivers better-quality information to me and the management team.

From that weekly response, I am able to work with the management team very quickly to respond and adjust, if need be. Here are some of questions we might ask, one at a time, in the weekly survey:

- What are you struggling with?
- Who in the company has been your rock star recently, and why?
- If you could change anything at the company, what would it be?

- What could you be doing better?
- How could we help our clients more?
- What do we do well?
- What is your biggest obstacle?
- What is your 'patronus'?

That last one, which refers to an animal guardian in the *Harry Potter* children's book series, is just for fun – an important part of any survey. Don't forget to have fun!

I have also experimented with sharing answers company wide (with advance notice) and with keeping them private to only me and a few senior managers. Both methods have pros and cons. I find the answers to private surveys to be more candid and in-depth. When we share the results with the whole company, people are more likely to limit what they share, either to protect their identity or to avoid upsetting or insulting someone. But, our company culture does benefit when everyone sees what everyone else wrote. People learn more about their co-workers and feel connected when others share their views. Overall, this helps them to be on the same page. Sharing also appears to spur conversations among team members towards solving problems, without any prompting by senior management. Since both approaches have benefits, I alternate between them every two or three months, each time informing my staff and managers how the survey question will be handled.

Of course, the 'right time' for collecting data varies by business and circumstance. Another simple process involves rating the company via the Net Promoter Score® (NPS), a numeric scale,– often from zero to 10 – on which customers perform a satisfaction self-assessment. The most well-known question from this type of survey is: 'How likely are you to recommend us to a friend?' On a scale of zero to 10, results are scored in groups: 0–6 are detractors; 7–8 are passive; and 9–10 are promoters – of whatever it is you are trying to measure. The goal is to get a rating of 9–10 from customers on each transaction or interaction.

This is a fabulous process, especially for companies in which the transaction is a product sale or a single interaction. We found this was not highly effective at PeopleG2, because our customers are ordering daily and have an ongoing service-based relationship. If your interactions are further apart, the NPS is a great tool. If you business is more like mine – a service and with a high level of interaction – give monthly surveys a try.

What to do with your results

Having all the relevant data in the world is great. But, how you interpret that data is more important. An effective analysis may allow you to check an immediate crisis, or it may influence your policy decisions for years to come. So, how should you go about classifying the answers you get and deciding whether or how to act on them? For example, suppose you get some negative remarks on a survey. You could stop asking the types of questions that provoked them. Or, you could value the fact that your respondents felt open enough to share their thoughts. Does this mean you should act only on the negative responses and ignore all the good things? Clearly not; but these are tough questions specific to your business that you and your team will need to grapple with.

The dangers in interpretation – even of numeric data – are the opportunities for subjective or agenda-promoting reasoning and, of course, our many cognitive biases. Let's talk for a moment about how to get a clearer picture from the information we collect.

Interpret wisely

The work of two prominent psychologists, Amos Tversky and Daniel Kahneman, who specialized in studying cognitive bias and behavioural economics, sheds light on the inherent problems and potential solutions in data analysis. Author Michael Lewis of *Moneyball* fame, in his book *The Undoing Project*,[5] discusses the results of a study by Tversky and Kahneman that bears on our understanding of these concepts. They found that people were likely to believe even suspect data from a small group or sample size and would attempt to rationalize the things that did not make sense.

The hypothesis in question was whether people with long noses lie more often than those with short noses. Data to back this up might, without suggesting a true correlation, reveal a group heavy on long-nosed liars and another group in which the short-noses lied more frequently. The question that Tversky and Kahneman studied was how *psychologists* would interpret this information. Did biases play into *their* findings?

The answer was yes. Instead of adjusting the sample size, judging the data inconclusive, or using other options, most psychologists surveyed preferred to find a correlation or another explanation for the variance between the two 'nose' groups. By trying to find an explanation to explain the difference they were attempting rationalize the data.

So how do we defend against this happening, when groups of highly educated psychologists kept making the error? The answer is to gather *more* data. Make sure your sample size is large enough, before you start drawing any conclusions. If the findings diverge between small groups, you need more data in order to be sure. Here is a simple explanation of why this is true.

If I ask 10 of my employees to tell me their favourite food, and 6 out of 10 say tacos, that does not mean that tacos are the preferred food at the company. In fact, I am unlikely to get the same result as I expand my survey and get more data. If I ask a second group of 10 employees the same questions, and six of them say spaghetti, I have a conflict in the data. My first team prefers tacos, and my second team prefers spaghetti. But, maybe the first team regularly holds meetings at a Mexican restaurant. Or, perhaps the second team enjoyed some fantastic pasta at a group event. Clearly, I do not have enough data to know what food my employees overall prefer. I mean, where is the pizza? I might find, had I surveyed *all* of my employees, that pizza came up as a favourite more often than tacos and spaghetti.

Small sample sizes lead to poor conclusions. How you frame questions can also impact the results. Remember, humans think emotionally first, rationally second. Take into account the ways in which cognitive bias can invade your judgement. When you interpret your data make sure to:

- Gauge your sample size.

- If your data differs between groups, expand your sample size.

- Measure the same metrics frequently for greater insight (today it's pizza, but tomorrow it could be tacos).

- Measure the same metrics in different ways.

- Stay open to new outcomes over time.

- Don't make snap judgements based on *your* emotions.

Include measurement in daily ops

As you discover the sheer effectiveness of tracking employee and business performance and acting on the results, you will want to integrate the practice fully into your day-to-day operations. You may already have ideas on how to do this in your company, or you may devote an entire sector of your management to it, as so many successful companies do. My favourite way to get and interpret data, and to implement strategies based on that analysis, is through a system.

A system of execution sets up a broad framework that gives everyone in the organization the tools needed to move measurement into a habit and findings into practice. At PeopleG2, this drives how we work, when we meet and how we get better. Popular philosophies that show how to customize a system include Six Sigma, Lean and Waterfall, efficiency methodologies that were first developed in the 1980s. You will find copious resources for researching these support programmes, so I'll take this opportunity to describe the system that works for us at PeopleG2: it's called Scrum, also known as Agile.

Scrum is a project management system that was originally designed for software development. Its name conjures images of a hard-fought rugby match, a mix of effort and strategy that translates perfectly to business performance. When I set out to write this book, I enrolled in a Scrum certification course that truly sold me on its value. My IT team uses it every day for every interaction and decision they make. But, Scrum will also serve any project-based initiative you have. Here's how it works.

The Scrum formation consists of rotating interdepartmental teams focused on the same project goals. Each team is led by a 'scrum master', who acts in the traditional role of project manager, and a 'product owner' who gets the big picture on what the team hopes to achieve and directs it accordingly. The team, which is largely autonomous from central management, decides what to do, estimates the depth and difficulty level of each task, and monitors their pace and progress as they go. They systematically perform the background work, and once they are ready to start, they 'sprint'. Over time, everyone takes turns being the scrum master, and the timing of sprints is staggered among teams. This gives individuals new perspectives and keeps them from burning out before objectives are reached.

Since people cannot participate in more than one sprint at a time, they get built-in relief from intense projects. This is not just an opportunity for rest and relaxation. Sometimes we need to fall back, plan, rethink and strategize. This is a nice balance that helps companies to focus attention on project implementation and improvements in manageable bursts.

Our projects tend to have one-week sprints, for two to three weeks in a row. Every Monday morning, we have a 15-minute planning meeting to decide who is working on what, and how much work we think we can get done that week. We answer questions like, *What did I do yesterday? What will I do today? Which obstacles are getting in my way?* The scrum master uses answers to these questions to dictate what happens next.

This short consultation is amazingly effective for every participant. It is transparent, it is centred around communication, and it clearly measures individual and group progress. You have to tell your peers what you have done, so you make sure tasks are completed. You see how your team members are progressing each day. When obstacles arise, it is easy to see what you can do to help others.

At the end of a sprint, the team meets in retrospect. They talk about what worked, what they might have done differently, and what they can do next time to improve. This is another form of real-time measurement, one that is dynamic and fully relevant to company operations. It can even serve to 'measure' a measurement tactic, such as the process of performing a customer service survey.

Whether you choose Scrum or another formal methodology, or whether you institute a more casual system that is specific to your business, do check the pulse of your operations on a regular basis. Do find a well-structured means of implementing decisive action based on your data analysis. These opportunities for damage control and advancement should not be relegated to an annual schedule. After all, you must conduct business – and support team culture – year round.

Pillar III review

What value does measurement hold for company cultures?

Using objective means of collecting data, analysing its importance and implementing resulting solutions brings teams together, rather than dividing them by casting blame. Sharing results encourages individuals to account for their own progress while recognizing that of others.

What should companies focus on measuring? How and when should they do it?

Tightly focus on KPIs known to affect the success and failure of your business. Assessments can record performance after the fact, as with customer satisfaction surveys or employee reviews, or they can track in-progress activities such as website hits measured by computer analytics. Frequent, periodic evaluation affords comparative and ongoing insights.

How can measurement be incorporated into routine business operations?

Make data collection and analysis an integral part of your operational framework by using short weekly surveys or a project-management system such as Scrum.

Notes

1 Bock, L (2015) *Work Rules! Insights from inside Google that will transform how you live and lead*, Hachette Book Group, New York

2 IBM (2017) [accessed 23 July 2017] Watson In Healthcare [Online] http://www-03.ibm.com/innovation/us/watson/watson_in_healthcare.shtml

3 Work (2017) [accessed 13 May 2017] The five keys to a successful Google team [Online] https://rework.withgoogle.com/blog/five-keys-to-a-successful-google-team/

4 Harvard Business Review (2013) [accessed 20 May 2017] The impact of employee engagement on performance [Online] https://hbr.org/resources/pdfs/comm/achievers/hbr_achievers_report_sep13.pdf

5 Lewis, M (2016) *The Undoing Project*, W.W. Norton, New York

Pillar IV: acknowledgement 06

We have begun our cultural foundation with important pillars – transparency, positivity and measurement. That's a lot of heavy lifting. You've earned the opportunity to work on a feelgood element of workplace culture, one that is fairly simple to incorporate: acknowledging good work. This pillar naturally supports the others, making them worth all the effort.

In our private lives, acknowledgement takes many forms: student honour rolls, community service awards, and personal pats on the back from those who appreciate our achievements. At work, we are familiar with Employee of the Month credits, prizes for meeting sales goals and, of course, the yearly cash bonus. These last three markers illustrate the two main types of staff acknowledgement: **recognition based** and **reward based**. Recognition-based acknowledgement publicly honours the performer by letting others know of their accomplishments. This system uses praise as compensation for extra effort. Reward-based acknowledgement remunerates the performer with something of value for having succeeded. This system uses money or something else the receiver values as compensation.

In this chapter, we will delve deeply into why workplace acknowledgement is a key part of culture. We will look at the pros and cons of the two approaches for acknowledging performance, and discuss some practical ways on how to implement the best ones at your company.

Incentives are important

We hire people and keep them on with the expectation that they will strive to do their jobs well. Since employees already work for pay and benefits, why offer them additional acknowledgement? Because it makes them more engaged in what they are asked to do every day. Let's get real: workplace acknowledgement is not just a way of being 'nice' to staff members. It exists as an added incentive to furthering company goals.

Here is another way to think about the topic. We ask employees to accept and act on the company's mission, values and vision – ideals that they may not fully espouse or prioritize outside the workplace. We ask them to do this in order to create a cohesive culture devoted to advancing the company interests, which are, first, to be profitable – otherwise there is no company – and second, everything else we wish our enterprises to accomplish. These requests are additional to all of the tasks that an individual's job might require. A little extra credit every now and then can't hurt, and it might be just the compensation needed to keep everyone on board.

Who doesn't like to hear praise? It's constructive and speaks to the practice of emphasizing what works well instead of focusing on problems. It fits right in with our goal of injecting positivity into group dynamics. Let's look at why acknowledgement has value, and how it plays an integral part in good company culture.

Why humans crave acknowledgement

When we think of awards and bonuses, we tend to think about the payoff for whoever is on the receiving end. But acknowledgement is not a one-way street. The receiver gains praise, but the givers and observers have much to gain as well. Recognizing the virtues of other people removes the tendency to focus on oneself, and encourages outreach and connection.

A culture of acknowledgement, then, might prompt new outlooks on performance. In an article for *Fast Company* magazine, David Mayer, associate professor of management at the University of Michigan and faculty member at the Center for Positive Organizations, eloquently suggests that instead of asking 'How can I improve?' the better question might be, 'How can I start seeing more of the good in people, more often?'[1] Mayer concludes that seeing the good in others may have a greater impact on us – and our happiness at work – than constantly fixating on our own behaviours.

When I read this, the idea captivated me. I immediately recalled hundreds of happy interactions among my employees sparked by regular and persistent acknowledgement of and by their peers. In a massive kaleidoscope of memories, I can easily picture their smiles, from both the people giving and receiving kudos. I know that we all enjoy this sort of exchange but I wanted to know why. I was fascinated to learn that acknowledgement situations build trust, something that helped early humans to develop group systems, and something that we highly prize today.

Mayer describes this concept by citing University of Georgia research, which showed that people who usually trust others at work tend to score higher in performance and have a higher commitment to the team than those who are more distrustful. What does this have to do with acknowledgement? Plenty. The two are linked, and this helps us to overcome yet another bias that humans carry – an **incentives bias** – one that results in a double standard.

We tend to assume that our own motivations are intrinsic or honourable. *I work because I love to do a good job*, we tell ourselves. Yet, we tend to assume that other people operate from base motivations – that they are only doing their jobs because they get paid. These were the collective findings of four different studies by Duke University researchers into incentive biases.[2] Of all the mental baggage we bring to work, instinctively mistrusting our peers is among the most damaging. It's amazing we ever get anything done. Of course, the human race would never have evolved if this preconception did not soften over time.

Fortunately, as we rub elbows with people, we start to see them in a different light. They prove to us that they can be trusted, maybe by communicating shared values, fulfilling promises, or mutually respecting certain qualities. But this organic method is time consuming, and only works to bring us closer to people within our personal circles. As Mayer says, what we need is to trust more people. The best way to do this on a wide scale is through acknowledgement.

Public recognition can positively affect opinions without the need to personally interact with the recipients. How might this work for you? Suppose that Sharon, a co-worker whom you trust, recognizes Joe for helping her meet an important deadline. Joe works in another department and you don't know him. So, let's say she posts this in the company newsletter. Joe's visibility and credibility just went up. Now you know who he is and believe you might trust him. But, if Sharon had only sent Joe an e-mail to thank him, instead of sharing that information in the newsletter, that trust boost would be lost on you.

We need these interactions to expand beyond our natural prejudices about abilities and those around us – to move past a fixed mindset. Acknowledgement is also vital to our personal well-being. Most of us like to be recognized. We like people to respect our work ethic, ingenuity and skill at what the company is paying us to do. We want our bosses to know that we can be trusted, and our co-workers to know that we are competent and motivated. We want to feel good about what we do, beyond what we are being paid. Where does that lead company leaders? To incentive programmes.

Recall from Daniel Pink's work mentioned in Chapter 2 that monetary incentives can be problematic – that they work well as rewards for performing mechanical tasks but not as well in work requiring more complex mental exertion. Of course, companies do use cash and prizes to acknowledge good performance from time to time. In fact, I'll tell you later on how the Las Vegas casino operator Caesars Entertainment benefits from that system. But many other businesses use nonmonetary incentives, or blend the two. Before we discuss the options, let's look into elements of acknowledgement that everyone needs to incorporate, no matter which delivery system you choose.

Best practices

You may be surprised to know that giving verbal or written acknowledgement is all you really must do to make someone's day. This does not mean that managers need to start following their direct reports around and complimenting their employees' every move. Neither do they have to 'give' rewards, although, if they do, they should not expect anything in return. Sincere acknowledgement should be an incentive, not a bribe or blackmail.

Still, it is possible to give too much or not enough – or for praise to ring hollow or become a burden when institutionalized. So, what is appropriate praise, and what form makes it the most meaningful? We will answer that in light of each of these best acknowledgement practices, which will make any programme work:

1 **Peer-to-peer acknowledgement** should take priority. Find opportunities for the majority of recognition exchanges in your company to come from co-workers, rather than management. Saying thank you to people on your team or other teams has a greater reciprocal effect than top-down praise that is compromised by the power relationship.

2 **Top-down acknowledgement** should be issued regularly but not dominate the recognition process. Open up less numerous but more memorable exchange opportunities for managers to show their appreciation for excellent work.

3 **Reciprocal acknowledgement** creates a positivity spiral with no end. Invite two-way recognition through '360-degree reviews', or surveys between managers and direct reports. This eliminates the appearance of staff praising bosses to gain favour, and gives management the chance to enjoy their 15 minutes of fame.

4 **Acknowledgement mechanisms** can instil the practice into company culture without making it onerous for the group. Take the time to recognize individuals and teams at existing lunches or meetings, have

brag boards, or feature outstanding employees at special events such as company-wide holiday parties or picnics.

5 **Measurement and acknowledgement** make terrific partners. Did you receive great reviews on surveys or increase profitability? Let everyone know. Discover what is working, through data analysis, and celebrate a team effort.

Sources of recognition

The first three best practices have to do with which way the good news is flowing. Let's talk a little bit about why the source of acknowledgement is important. First, why should we elicit more praise from staff versus management? This is all about empowerment, a key to employee autonomy. When your staff take responsibility for acknowledging their own, it is revolutionary. I watched this positive change in action following my company's dark days of 2009. (We will get to the details in the PeopleG2 example in the next section, 'Recognition-based systems'.)

Besides those two ways to sing praises – from the bottom up and top down, which carry different degrees of influence – a reciprocal opportunity to acknowledge the best work of both parties comes in the form of 360-degree reviews. This refers to the full-circle nature of a survey conducted across teams, or between managers and direct reports.

In this more egalitarian context, managers get their due respect and appreciation from staff, and vice versa. With both sides reporting, employees feel safe in being candid about a manager, since they expect the same treatment. This type of review serves acknowledgement purposes and gathers valuable data for HR and department managers. They can learn when bosses effectively helped, supported or mentored staff members – information they can cross-reference against performance metrics to drive a variety of decisions.

Mechanisms and measurement

We have already talked about many mechanisms your company can implement to encourage acknowledgement situations, and you will come up with more ideas. Positive measurement outcomes offer another chance to create acknowledgement mechanisms. Like 360-degree reviews, measurement-prompted recognition reaps dual benefits: besides using data to identify top performers, you can use this practice to forward your company's brand.

We have all seen advertisements, press releases, blog posts and articles promoting good news by businesses. Some pay for space or submit features about the company or individual employees gaining notoriety – such as a reporter winning a Pulitzer Prize, an advertiser winning a new high-visibility client, or a developer promoting a cutting-edge invention. You can generate your own opportunities for self-praise by sharing great outcomes that you have measured. Noteworthy profits, growth, customer satisfaction – or whatever you track and analyse – are fair game. These are things you can extol internally, on the company website, or in national or international news venues.

Now that you have got these general best practices, let's look into the mechanisms behind recognition-based acknowledgement, the most effective form of tribute that any company can employ – to everyone's advantage.

Recognition-based systems

Daniel Pink's work on mastery, autonomy and purpose provides the best reasons to get behind recognition-based acknowledgement. Recall that his research found that money, prizes and pay rises detract from employees having the big three in their work and lives. A 2010 collaboration between the employer group WorldatWork, Loyola University and Hay Group underscores that assertion. Their survey of more than 700 WorldatWork members revealed that 'base pay and benefits had the overall weakest relationship with the organization's ability to foster high levels of employee engagement and motivation compared to incentives, intangible rewards and quality of leadership'.[3]

Because this last element – good leaders – showed the strongest correlation with employee motivation, the researchers recommended using monetary incentives to attract effective managers. Their advice for motivating staff echoed Pink's: 'Think in terms of total rewards and not just financial rewards. Develop employee engagement resources that are directed towards work environment or organization climate, work–life balance and the nature of the job and quality of the work, and career opportunities.' In other words, efforts that meet shared human needs represent strong potential motivators for workers on the ground.

To understand why this might be the case, let's examine Maslow's hierarchy of needs, a model designed by respected US psychologist Abraham Maslow.[4] He considered five fundamentals necessary to psychological well-being, which he illustrated in pyramid fashion, each one building on the last. I'll flip that imagery for you here, putting our greatest needs first; they are:

---

1 Physiological needs

2 Safety

3 Love/belonging

4 Esteem

5 Self-actualization

Whether we are at home or work, these basics must be met in order for us to enjoy mental health and be motivated to reach our individual potential. The quick explanation for their order is that, before meeting our internal desires, we first must satisfy our physical requirements.

We all share a human drive for items one and two above: to eat, drink, breathe, have a place to sleep, and not have a bear waiting to eat us if we step outside. Note that these easily translate to the workplace. It is hard to focus if you are too hungry, thirsty or tired. Safety, in this environment, is relative – it can mean being physically free from harm or free to perform work without reprisals. This is an area that I hear business speakers talk a lot about. If your employees don't feel 'safe', they cannot move along to fulfil their other needs and do their best.

A quest for love and belonging in our personal lives is easy to understand. At work, this really resonates in the quality of company culture. Workplace interaction is inherently social – it is where we form friendships and feel accepted. Companies with good culture find ways to foster friendships and a sense of community, which discourages the formation of cliques and gossip channels. Making open communication a clear priority is a good start.

This brings us to the stage most relevant to our current topic – for esteem is clearly supported through acknowledgement of individual skill and effort. Maslow defines the search for esteem as a wish to feel confident in our abilities and respected by others, which in turn, causes us to find reasons to respect other people.

Having fulfilled all of these burning human desires, in the right circumstances, we are able to achieve self-actualization. This is what company leaders are looking for: self-motivation to employ creativity, problem solving, openness to new ideas and facts, morality and spontaneity. It is a nice coincidence that employees want the chance to express those things.

Maslow held that these latter urges could not be satisfied without fulfilling the others first. On its face, his theory makes a lot of sense. If you constantly worry about when your next meal will come or where you will sleep tonight, it is tough to think about being creative, or to do your part in relationships with family or friends. In the 50-plus years since Maslow aired these views, the scientific community has questioned his lack of empirical evidence and the interdependent hierarchy of these needs. That's okay; the basic model still works, and the new understanding lets business and HR leaders address things that employees intrinsically want as opportunities arise – particularly when it comes to recognition.

Whether you speak or write about an individual's outstanding efforts, formally acknowledging good work is a boon to company culture. Think of it as a pep rally that everyone can attend. Everyone has a chance to both receive and witness accolades, which builds trust and a more intimate network among your staff. Now, here's the story of how we worked this practice into our business operations at PeopleG2, plus a few more practical ways to recognize employees at your company.

CASE STUDY   The green flag system at PeopleG2

To open up channels for recognition at our company, I followed some advice about public acknowledgement from Kim Shepherd of Decision Toolbox. This resulted in the mechanism that we still use today.

As a remote company in which everyone works from home or a different location, PeopleG2 uses an online communication program called HipChat to stay in touch on matters big and small. Like Slack and other instant-messaging programs, it allows our people to stay connected one-on-one, as well as in virtual group 'rooms' where teams or the entire company can log in and participate. When we started this program, I created a chat room called The Water Cooler. It's an open forum where staff are invited to talk about anything at all, if it is work appropriate, and where we say thank you publicly. To highlight these acknowledgements, we use what we call a 'green flag', one of our mechanisms for recognition.

Here's how it works: we created a computer emoji, or stylized image, of a green flag. When people want to shout out co-workers' contributions, they add this icon to their Water Cooler message, and say things like, 'A big green flag to Bryan for helping with a client question I didn't know how to answer.' Or, the announcement acknowledges help with a heavy workload or training expertise. This recognition comes from a peer, but then everyone in the company who signs in to this chat room also posts thanks, applause or other well wishes.

That is where the magic happens. It feels so good to have dozens of people congratulate you. As I mentioned earlier, this reinforces your trust in others and in the reliability of the company – in other words, your good deeds will not go unnoticed. With a little encouragement, staff members green-flag each other of their own accord. Occasionally, someone will give a green flag to a manager, or vice versa, but we ask that managers curb their urge to do so, since we find the practice to be most powerful peer to peer.

We explain the nuances of the green flag to new hires and we try to ensure that managers don't go overboard with top-down public praise, not because it is bad, but because people start expecting it to come from the top, and not from each other.

If your company has a traditional office space, you could also do this through e-mail blasts, a company newsletter or in a physical meeting. Think of using fun props or fanfare, if your team is physically together in an office. Let your employees take the reins on this most of the time. You don't have to track instances, but shoot for a balance like an 80/20 per cent split. Make it easy for staff to give shout-outs. Managers should focus their praise less frequently and more formally, such as in personal e-mails, letters, reviews, etc, which can then be reposted. Top-down acknowledgement gains significance when it is rare and when your boss puts it in writing and delivers it directly to you.

Reward-based systems

Verbal kudos sent among co-workers are concrete tokens of esteem, and not to be discounted. But, what about those times when it is more appropriate or meaningful to present a gift or physical tribute? Your company culture may be such that award ceremonies or retirement parties naturally incorporate giving into an acknowledgement system. Special recognition circumstances, such as significant impacts on the community or lifetime achievement, may warrant rewards and not be a detriment to motivation. After all, community service bears its own purposeful incentive, and outbound retirees no longer need one.

Giving, however, has its own caveats. A gift that is not meaningful may have the opposite effect that rewards should create. Suppose you want to award something of value to an exceptional performer. Do so in a personalized way – not a personal way, which might be inappropriate or misinterpreted, but in a way that forms a human connection.

For example, suppose you want to offer a small gift to your employee, Don, for staying late to do inventory. Giving him a $5 coffee-shop gift card is so generic that it makes no individual connection. It says, *Wow, Your Name Here, the work you did was amazing. Here is a card with only $5 on it*. You can barely buy a blended drink for that. Instead, if you learn what Don's favourite drink is, at the next team meeting you can announce Don's awesomeness to the group and hand him the drink that you picked up yourself. The impact is totally different. It's not the price of the coffee, it's the thought that counts. Don gets that warm, fuzzy feeling from your effort to get to know him and to praise him in front of the group, by name. In the end, Don gets the same drink. But the approach and outcome has a much deeper effect, on both Don and on your office culture, in general.

Below is another, real-life example to show you how pairing measurement with recognition helps to ensure you are acknowledging everyone, and not just the extroverts who easily gain attention. Kim Shepherd of Decision Toolbox came up with an ingenious way to use this objective tool.

Decision Toolbox is an HR recruiting company, so Shepherd wanted a reward-based means of managing recruitment accounts based on performance numbers. Her team developed a system to track employee-driven KPIs such as candidate placement times, customer satisfaction ratings and industry expertise. When new candidates sign on with the company, the recruiters with the best records get first pick of the new jobs. If you are the fastest recruiter with the best customer satisfaction ratings, you will be first in line for accounts and opportunities to earn.

This is an objective form of recognition that relies on an algorithm to select those worthy of reward. Because all of Shepherd's recruiters know this, they have an equal incentive and opportunity to achieve it. They do not get the best work because they are nice, or friends with their manager, or happen to be at the right place at the right time. Their success at work is totally built on the measured responses of efficiency and satisfaction. Do you think that advances company culture? You bet!

CASE STUDY Caesars Entertainment

Now for an example on a grand scale. I had the good fortune of sharing the best reward-based acknowledgement programme I've come across with my radio-show listeners in 2015 on TalentTalk, when Terry Byrnes discussed how his corporation handles incentives.[5] Byrnes is vice president of Total Service at Caesars Entertainment, a vast hospitality and gaming empire that includes Caesars Palace casino, the World Series of Poker, and 40 US resorts. The company operates in 20 states and employs around 75,000 people. How do they motivate so many people in so many different types of jobs? They tie incentives to the quality of customer service they provide.

Byrnes says this system helps Caesars to give its customers a reason to choose their hotels based on service relationships with staff, rather than strictly on the price and special packages that drive this dense market. Byrnes's team analyses guest survey data to find correlations between customer ratings and brand loyalty. When a property exceeds a certain threshold target of good reviews and return business, every employee who works there is rewarded in bankable points called total return credits (TRCs). They can redeem these for quality merchandise such as electronics, on a sponsored website.

This programme is, indeed, motivating to hospitality workers whose salaries lean towards the bottom of the wage scale. Because these employees are the company's front line with customers, its substantial investment pays off. This year, the company will spend $8 million among 40,000 employees who achieve their targets. Byrnes told my radio audience that, despite a lull in the hospitality industry between 2008 and 2015, Caesars properties continued to lead in terms of customer satisfaction.

This type of incentive, backed by a strong investment, is good for business performance, and it is great for company culture. Caesars method of acknowledgement awards incentives for good results by the individual as well as the group at each property. This forges a bond with employees across the Caesars empire. Everyone knows what TRCs are, everyone wants them, and the whole staff find out when someone racks up record amounts of them for doing a good job.

Again, this system plays into the use of KPI data. The weekly totals from customer surveys are broadcast to front-line staff; these numbers, themselves, become incentives to try hard to win TRCs. They are also a metric that keep staff informed of how the company is doing, and give them a stake in it. Byrnes calls this weekly rhythm 'the sit-ups and push-ups' that allow the company to progress in a difficult market.

So, what is it worth – to the company and to staff? Since 2009, the company has spent $100 million in rewards as bankable points. Byrnes narrates the story of an employee in Illinois who accumulated TRCs worth almost $10,000 over the course of six years, which shows the value of the programme. 'We could have paid $100 million in cash', Byrnes pointed out, 'but I think we got more value by paying it in bankable points. People attach accomplishment to the reward, and when they redeem it for an iPad, or something for the kids, or a barbeque grill, it becomes a memory they connect to their achievement at work, and it extends it to the family experience.'

In this case, I think you will have to agree that Caesars uses monetary rewards to help fulfil some of the basic needs described by Daniel Pink and Abraham Maslow. You don't have to have the market presence of Caesars Entertainment to enact such a programme. Consider it an exercise in finding the best way to acknowledge your staff's good deeds. Be creative and apply Byrnes's lessons on a smaller scale, using features that suit your company.

Pillar IV review

How do the best acknowledgement practices enhance company culture?

Acknowledging employees publicly fills basic human needs, which include gaining trust with other people and improving their self-esteem. This gives employees the motivation to perform well – individually and as a team – and to unite with co-workers behind the company's mission, values and vision.

What are some recognition-based approaches to acknowledgement?

Giving verbal accolades and thanks in meetings, lunches, ceremonies and other gatherings is an opportunity for top performers to enjoy recognition while observers build trust in co-workers and the company. Recording achievements in print or digitally via company newsletters, e-mail or real-time chat rooms also engages the entire staff in the process.

What are the hallmarks of reward-based approaches to acknowledgement?

Tangible rewards can come in the form of cash, personalized gifts, service plaques or redeemable gift certificate or credits. Preferred treatment, such as first crack at the most desirable accounts, represents a nonmonetary reward that still holds great value for employees.

Notes

1 Mayer, D (2017) [accessed 28 May 2017] Want to be happier and more successful? Learn to like other people, *Fastcompany.com* [Online] https://www.fastcompany.com/40401630/want-to-be-happier-and-more-successful-learn-to-like-other-people

2 Science Direct (1999) [accessed 28 May 2017] On the social psychology of agency relationships: Lay theories of motivation overemphasize extrinsic incentives [Online] http://www.sciencedirect.com/science/article/pii/S0749597899928261

3 Scott, D and McMullen, T (2010) [accessed 28 May 2017] The impact of rewards programs on employee engagement, Worldatwork.org [Online] https://www.worldatwork.org/adimLink?id=39032

4 Maslow, A (1954) *Motivation and Personality*, Harper, New York

5 TalentTalk (2015) [accessed 29 May 2017] Susan Steinbrecher and Terry Byrnes [Online] http://www.talenttalkradio.com/e/susan-steinbrecher-and-terry-byrnes-12152015/

Pillar V: uniqueness

07

Does company culture make our businesses unique? Or do our business practices make workplace culture unique? Both of these things are true, and it is the shared nature of the relationship that makes working on your company's culture so satisfying. As culture gains character, your business image sharpens. As your brand grows stronger, your staff's group dynamic follows suit. This helps people work together more effectively, and makes working for your company pleasant, or cool, or exciting – which draws great talent to your team.

I think you can see where I'm going with this. All of these things affect daily operations and your business's bottom line. Therefore, the things that make your brand and your company culture unique tremendously influence your revenue and market standing. Yes, this is why we are working on culture and this is why, right now, we are discussing the importance of uniqueness within an organization.

To that end, think about what you hear in the halls or meeting rooms of your company. If you have put the pillars of transparency, positivity and acknowledgement in place, your staff should enjoy open, constructive communication. Including your team members in the measurement process gives them a common pool of objective terminology, so you might hear people talking about surveys that are under way or the results of those ratings and how they are meeting goals and targets. This shared language is unique to your company and a direct driver of culture. It is worth some special attention.

So, let's give it some, and uncover the mysteries of the role of speech in the complex interplay between company and culture. In this chapter, we will work in the same sort of circular motion that accompanies that relationship. We will talk in more depth about the benefits of having a distinct culture, how to rate your company's degree of individuality, and how language may be the defining factor in both of those realms.

Workplace uniqueness

Your workplace – including the people in it – is where culture resides. Your company's unique combination of its social atmosphere and business ethos exists for a common purpose, which gives every member of the team a reason to return every day to fulfil that purpose. Again, the reciprocal nature of business transaction and business culture is self-perpetuating, as long as your business thrives.

Purpose, then, is paramount in injecting uniqueness into workplace culture. Recall Simon Sinek's view in Chapter 1 that, when it comes to an impetus to work hard, our 'why' is even more important to us than money. On a company level, it is the reason that we, as an enterprise, exist. On an employee level, it is why we believe in the company deeply enough to try to do our jobs well. Knowing and understanding this key concept not only focuses us as an organization, but allows our clients to understand our services in a meaningful way.

So, it is first our collective 'why' that makes a culture unique. Then come the 'what' and 'how' – what we, together, make or do and how we do it. These defining areas make up our cultural identity. Suppose we make pencils. We make them using the most efficient technology available, keeping prices low. That is what and how, but why do we make pencils? What is our vision, our pencils' contribution to the world? Perhaps it is: 'XYZ Pencils makes quality, affordable writing instruments to ensure that every child has the tools to participate in their education.' This 'why' brings our purpose into focus.

Depending on your business sector, those who work for you may or may not have a say in what they make or do. But there are still opportunities to exercise unique skills or ideas in *how* those things come together. This 'how' is the icing on the culture cake, as it reveals the subtle differences in who you are as an organization while you work.

None of these ideals are carried out without people. To start building a unique company culture, you have got to attract – and keep – strong talent. In Chapter 2, I encouraged you to welcome diversity of thought in your workforce. Yes, this makes for animated brainstorming sessions and novel solutions. But it also, naturally, injects unique personalities into your workplace – people whose energy adds to a collective momentum that carries everyone through the day and on to the next challenge.

So, how can you honour individual identity and integrate these outstanding people into your existing culture? By *defining your uniqueness* for those you wish to hire. If you can design a recruiting process to ensure that your new hires fit your culture and will thrive in your culture, the organization will benefit from 'talent reputation'. This is the best free publicity you can get – companies known for having top people are the places that everyone wants to work. In the United States, think of Google, Nike and Amazon. It's not just impressive campuses, free meals and dog-friendly offices that draw the best. Those things are nice, but at the same time those HR departments are very, very good at finding the right people who will flourish in their companies.

Remember the DISC Profile we discussed in Chapter 3? If you have surveyed your staff for their motivating traits, you have insight into what kind of people do well within your culture and day-to-day operations. Does your company have other ways of deciding how to build on your team's strengths or fill voids? At PeopleG2, my question-a-week survey also helps me to understand more about how my employees think and what makes them unique. This is what I call 'their story'. Let's find out what happens when we put together the various narratives behind every team member.

Employee uniqueness

As new clients vet you and talent considers joining your company, they are looking for ways to know and understand you better. By highlighting some of the similarities and strengths in your workforce – each of whom has their own story – you give a broad account of your company. Think of this as a collage. It is made up of many small pictures to form a larger work of art. It uses parts to more greatly define a whole. Similarly, finding brand uniqueness through your employees can be a rewarding and effective strategy.

So, look for unique hallmarks and unifying passions among two groups: your current employees and potential employees. Start with the people who work for you. What are their areas of mastery, on the job and outside of work? Is there a way that one reflects on the other? If so, it could point you towards the story you need to tell in order to stand out.

For example, if you have 10 employees and eight of them coach youth sports, you now have a story centred on leadership, giving back to the community, and common interests. You can use this story to gain visibility in local newspapers or on your company's website or social media pages.

Your staff might contribute time, effort or goods to everything from food banks and dog shelters to community theatre and fundraising events. Large companies could look into all the volunteering done by staff and use the sheer volume of hours as a way to differentiate themselves. A company with 100 employees who volunteer an average of 10 hours a month could develop content around the 1,000 hours its staff is investing in the community each month. Putting together this story of giving and support costs nothing, other than the effort to figure it out. In garnering public recognition, job candidates might notice that you reflect their interests and decide your company would be a great place to work.

Asking your staff to share their personal pursuits brings all of you closer together, and we know that this type of engagement is a good thing. In 2017, Gallup released its updated findings on the state of the modern workplace.[1] They surveyed more than 31 million clients and employees to learn what is important to them and how well their needs are satisfied. When their needs are met, the study shows, workers tend to stick with the company. Engagement, however, is still a major issue, with only 33 per cent in the workforce saying they are engaged. Among Gallup's qualifiers for employee engagement are:

- feeling their opinions count;
- being cared about as a person;
- having the chance to do what they do best every day.

These qualifiers have everything to do with appreciating employees' uniqueness, and the most successful companies are doing that. Within what Gallup terms the 'world's best organizations', data showed engagement levels of 70 per cent. If potential job holders knew that about your company, some great CVs would come flooding in. Suppose you measured your employee engagement levels independently and used the results all over your website's Careers page. Would that help or hurt your company at the present moment?

Many companies fail to create a truly dynamic online presence to demonstrate where they are unique, and which employees would be best suited at their company. You can streamline your recruiting process by being both creative and specific in this area. Even if you are not able to pay top dollar, you can draw in accomplished candidates by showing them why your company culture is attractive and how they will fit into it.

Brand uniqueness

The whole purpose of branding is to set businesses apart from the competition – to position them as uniquely able to fulfil customers' needs. But, as we are seeing, branding has the nice side effect of delineating a company's culture. As you delve into this subject, you will naturally come up with a list of things that your company does best. Then, all you have to do is show that you do them better than everyone else.

Your unique selling points

You will find incredible value in discovering the large and small things that make your organization unique. Like identifying your KPIs in the service of measuring your company's progress, finding your unique selling points (USPs) is a key to linking your brand to your workplace culture. Is your business a game changer in the marketplace? Is it one of many stalwarts in a sea of commodities? Either type of enterprise has something special to bring to its brand, thanks to the uniqueness of any workforce and the particular vision that its leaders champion.

If you don't think that is true across the board, let's return to the hypothetical XYZ Pencils company. Let's suppose you own the factory, and all it does is make medium-grade graphite pencils – the yellow, wooden kind with an orange eraser on top. There may be dozens of manufacturers of these things around the world. What would make you unique in the marketplace? How could you describe what makes your company and your product different to potential customers, distributors or employees?

Utilitarian pencils are the perfect example of a commoditized product. Buyers give little to no concern about its finer points; what they care about is the price, because they assume that pencils are all the same. How much a box of pencils costs, and how many come in a box, are their USPs.

Let's say that XYZ, Inc, based in Anytown, United States, is experiencing a fall-off in market share. Now is the time to sit down your employees in front of a whiteboard to identify what makes your product and company good and unique. They might come up with this list:

- made in USA;
- made in Anytown;
- nontoxic graphite lead and water-based paint;
- no toxic adhesives;
- better value/more in the box;
- eco friendly;
- great for art and school;
- designed for right- and left-handed people;

- family-owned and operated business for 100 years;
- female CEO;
- local charity connections;
- customer testimonials;
- employee stories;
- school stories.

It is true that your company might share some or all of these 14 items with other pencil companies. But, we're not finished yet. From these main differentiators may come small but significant ones. Suppose your lack of poisonous glues in the manufacturing process becomes big news in the wake of a pencil-materials scandal that sickens scores of schoolchildren. You can capitalize on that. Or, maybe the closure of family-owned businesses overall gives the rest greater attention. You can promote your staying power.

The value here is both in the process of creating the list and finding which items generate the most excitement. Simple things that you and your staff have taken for granted for years might suddenly be revealed as USPs. Environmentally conscious employees might voice their appreciation for the company's contributions. Maybe you use wood made from cast-off lumber for your pencils. Maybe you use recycled packaging. After several people mention the value of these USPs, your company might make donations to conservation groups, and mention this gesture in advertising spots or print it on the pencil boxes.

Once you have your main USPs listed, take each one apart to see whether more ideas come to mind. Your company has been in business for a century! What has changed in the writing implement world during that time? You can show all the forks in the road that other companies took, and thus, point out another differentiator: XYZ Pencils stayed the same. No one ever built a 'better mouse trap'. As you drill down to find more evidence of your organization's uniqueness, be sure to look outward: at your clients.

Client uniqueness

Buried in the fourteen-point list above lies a very important source for USPs: customer testimonials. Things that are unique to your company include not just the product, how it was made and who made it – but which *customers* you reach out to. Take some time to review exactly who your distributors and end users are. This will tell you if you are missing a target market that might put the company back on track.

After brainstorming with staff, start surveying your clients. Who are the intermediaries who purchase your goods and get them into stores, homes and offices? They can give you ideas that might not occur to you. A good place to focus is on accounts that have been with you for the longest and shortest periods of time. Those with a long association can tell you why they have been clients for so long, and how they view your relationship. They might even relate a success story or a specific event that illustrates the relationship. Conversely, new accounts can also provide valuable information. Asking them to articulate why they chose you, as it is fresh in their minds, could uncover stories or differences you had taken for granted.

Defining a specific segment of a marketplace has been a proven strategy to win business and differentiate yourself. For example, if we head back to your pencil company, we could use some segmented approaches to play up XYZ's uniqueness. First, you could choose a single segment and focus your sales efforts on it completely – let's say, schools. Marketing, distribution and sales devote themselves to what schools want and need. This allows you to add to your marketplace conversation: 'We specialize in pencils for schools!'

Now you have an image as experts, and the licence to expand campaigns where schools could benefit. You could use the Warby Parker model discussed in Chapter 2 and donate a box of pencils to children in need, for every box sold. You could seek an endorsement by professional groups or related businesses, such as teacher's organizations or test-prep companies. By becoming the official pencil company for a high-visibility group, you can service a specific market segment in a unique and powerful way.

Second, you could look to broaden your clientele. As the writing implement field has grown more sophisticated and diverse, consider who still uses sharpenable, nonmechanical pencils with black lead. How about crossword puzzle enthusiasts? Clearly scholars, writers and test proctors are additional groups. Is there someone among them who is well known, who might help promote the value of XYZ-style pencils? Perhaps a famous author or mathematician could be enlisted to share their pencil obsession.

Third, you could narrow your product offering to appeal to a basic but large client base. Suppose XYZ actually produces a modest range of pencils, with various lead thicknesses and hardness ratings, in a variety of fashion colours. But business has decreased. Now may be the time to move to a simplified offering – whatever your bestseller is. You can trumpet a return to the basic Number 2 model, in yellow, with an orange eraser. 'If that's what you need', clients will hear, 'look no further.'

Believe it or not, this approach does work for certain businesses. You are probably familiar with McDonald's, the world's biggest restaurant chain.[2]

When its first 'golden arches' franchise opened back in 1962, the company offered a limited lunch and dinner menu, largely renditions of hamburgers, French fries and milkshakes. Today, the chain's menu includes breakfast, desserts, salads and more than five dozen offerings. This expansion created a void in the market – a drive-in restaurant with *fewer* menu items.

Into this void stepped the US franchise In-N-Out Burger. This successful burger joint operates in a few regions and only sells a few items. If you want a burger, fries, a soda or a milkshake, you are in luck. But, if you want chicken or a salad, or any of the other things that McDonald's and its copycats sell, the In-N-Out won't have it. They just do what they do really well and keep it simple. That's their strategy for being unique and standing out in a competitive marketplace.

Even if none of these options for finding or increasing your company's unique qualities is quite right, your clientele can still show you in which direction your brand should head in order to make a comeback. It may be that adding to your product line will be the ticket. Be persistent in surveying your customers, whether by issuing a formal rating system or talking with account representatives in depth about what they like now, and what kind of merchandise they would like to see. It may be that your 100-year-old company can find new life by adding a unique, new spin-off on the old pencil theme to your catalogue.

When it comes to talking with your clients: there are a few more questions you should ask. Are you speaking their language? Or, better yet, are they speaking yours?

The role of unique language

The overall purpose of this pillar is to elevate your company culture by differentiating it from others – and to boost your business performance by owning those differences and letting people know about them. Besides the evaluative suggestions we have just walked through, another way to bring your staff together and stand out to your clients is to develop your own 'dialect'. When you encourage a certain line of discourse through your workforce, it can have a trickledown effect that may eventually reach the popular lexicon. Even if it stays within your office walls, you have created something that forms a bond among your team members and sets you apart from other companies that they could be working for.

I call this 'tribal speak'. Have you ever travelled and found yourself in a place whose main language you don't understand? It can be daunting. But, it can also be a fun part of the experience. What I find when I'm immersed in a foreign culture is what happens when I hear someone else speaking my language. Through all the indistinguishable chatter, if I hear English being spoken as I walk down a busy street, I am magically drawn to that speaker. We are intrinsically connected by our language in such instances, only because everyone else is not.

In this situation, total strangers easily ask each other all sorts of things – about where we live, our families, travel plans, suggestions for our next meal, etc. Transferring this language experience to the realm of work can make a significant impact on your culture. It can work both ways: to mark those who are part of it – 'insiders', or to invite outsiders in by sharing the language with them.

Company 'shorthand'

When someone comes from outside the company and does not understand your lingo, it reinforces the bond between you and your co-workers. You know something the other people don't. These speech mannerisms arise all the time in businesses that, by their nature, use special terminology – think the computer sector, marine products and services, or medical products manufacturers. One clear example of a more mainstream 'tribe' is retail giant Walmart. With over 11,000 stores worldwide and 2.5 million employees, their workforce is huge, and this is reflected in their culture. I learnt much about this from a visit to the Walmart Museum in Bentonville, Arkansas.

At the corporate level, Walmart employees have a very clear and intentional tribal speak. They use acronyms for everything. They use them with everyone connected with the company, from employees and vendors to contractors and distributors. Some of the acronyms are so long, I wondered whether they are worth using. But, this part of their culture makes them unique, and confers a sense of inclusion to those who understand and speak this letter-mash–filled language. For instance, HEATKTE (Pronounced HET-Ka-Tee) means *High Expectations Are The Key To Everything*. Then there is EDLP, which stands for *Every Day Low Price* (and which you are better off not trying to pronounce). Given Walmart's workforce size and market success, its 45-year journey from a single five-and-dime store to prominence holds lessons for culture seekers. Their internal language brings together individuals in the sprawling organization, reflecting the growth of culture on a vast scale.

Did Walmart leaders consciously institute their company 'shorthand'? Probably not. But once a common language begins to surface, it can be encouraged. You can also be on the lookout for opportunities for proprietary labelling. On a more intimate scale than Walmart's, for instance, you can create your own tribal speak around meetings, like we do at PeopleG2. Our approach to conferencing, and by extension, our terminology for it, is a source of great pride. As a completely virtual organization in which everyone works from remote locations, we need a lot of meetings to ensure communication and projects are effective. We speak by phone, Skype and online chat room, or in person, over lunch, if we feel the need and it is feasible. But we don't just have meetings for meetings' sake. That's not a good use of anyone's time.

To help me prioritize meetings and use our time most wisely, I again turned to Kim Shepherd of Decision Toolbox, who, along with Dave Berkus, co-wrote the helpful guide *Get Scrappy: Business insights to make your company more agile.*[3]

We adopted and expanded on their vocabulary and concepts to designate a hierarchy of consultations. At PeopleG2, everyone invited to a meeting knows how important it is and how critical their individual participation is – from optional to mandatory, and everything in between. The most frequent virtual gathering is called a 'cockroach meeting'. What's that? Imagine there is a cockroach in your bathroom. It's not a big deal, but it needs to be dealt with – possibly by a braver team member than yourself. When anyone in my company has a minor issue, they have the authority to call a cockroach meeting at any time.

When someone needs low-level input, they send out an e-mail or call to arms in the company room on our chat program, inviting anyone who can help to join in a cockroach meeting. It is up to the individual to describe the reason for the discussion, ensure they invite people who might be able to help, provide the conference phone number and run the meeting. This is so empowering to new employees, or anyone working on the front lines who is used to seeing a manager call and run a meeting. Cockroach meetings – as every team member learns – are voluntary. The purpose is simply to identify an issue and get several people together to talk about it. The benefits of these informal chats include: 1) quickly providing information to help the employee eliminate the obstacle; 2) gathering information and identifying who in the company would be the best person to approach for further help; and 3) moving the discussion to a team or a client, if greater attention is necessary. This process encourages anyone to raise their hand and ask for help or to let everyone in the company know that something – however small – is not right.

The next level up in significance or urgency is a 'tiger team meeting'. Again, if there was a tiger in your bathroom, it would be a fairly big deal. You would probably need specific help from certain highly trained people, plus a plan and a well-armed team to deal with this tiger. If we call a tiger team meeting, everyone knows to be prepared.

Our tiger team meetings are typically called by managers. They designate people to be on the mandatory call, as well as dole out any specific duties or research that need to be performed prior to the meeting. Tiger team meetings are meant to deal with big things that need planning and coordination to address. These conferences might be called for things like dealing with losing a large client, or preparing to woo a potential big account.

Another designation we use is an 'ostrich meeting'. Ostriches are famously misrepresented as timid birds that cope by putting their heads in the sand. For us, they are mascots for meetings in which one or more people need information, don't understand an issue, or just need help getting caught up with details. Again, anyone can call this meeting, and attendance is voluntary. I tend to convene these more than anyone else in our company. It is not uncommon for a project, new client or IT issue to become serious enough that the CEO's help is needed. When that happens, I find it perfect to call one of these meetings, and in 15 minutes allow everyone who has worked on the project to fill me in. They remind each other of facts and variables, and get me to a place where I can actually be effective. Try asking a few people to help you get your head out of the sand, and see how enthusiastically they respond. The pure acts of admitting you don't know something and requesting assistance are usually enough to get anyone talking.

The final term we use for conferencing is 'tsunami meeting'. We call for this level of meeting when an issue demands more strategic handling or long-term planning, and we often come together in person to get that work done. These concerns, if left unaddressed, could have a tidal-wave effect on the company. Key people relative to the issue are invited to get together and attempt to answer important, tsunami-level questions. For example, what would the company do if I was no longer able to function in my role? Are there any systems or processes where we don't have another executive in place who could conduct business if I were suddenly absent or incapacitated? In other words, am I the only person authorised to sign payroll cheques? I was, so we fixed that.

Another question we posed at a tsunami meeting was more upbeat and hypothetical: what if a large client came to us and increased our overall revenue by 50 per cent or more? It would be great to land that mega account, but how would we handle that? Do we have staff identified and key leadership to bring in? Would our current software and IT capabilities be sufficient, and could our vendors handle the increased workload? We found many simple, little- to no-cost solutions we could implement in order to be ready, just in case.

If you named your meetings or found other places in the organization to expand your tribal speak, imagine the impact it could have on your organization. These changes are fun and effective, and give you a story to tell your customers, employees, potential talent and vendors. They make your process unique and, by extension, your company culture.

Public buzzwords

If speaking a 'secret' language buoys staff intimacy, what happens when company-generated language goes public? Injecting your buzzwords into popular culture allows people who may not even be your customers to further your brand and your organization's unique culture. Wow. If ever there was free publicity, this is it.

Like Walmart, you can let your terminology seep into contacts with vendors and others connected to your business. They do it by flinging around those hip acronyms that practically beg people to ask what they stand for. Then, *they* start using them, perhaps in environments removed from business transactions as well. Do you have any elements of tribal speak that you share with vendors and clients? We might, if we invited a client to submit input via a tiger team meeting. (Discretion would probably keep us from inviting them to a cockroach meeting!)

Striking a buzz through public use of your company's shorthand will probably happen by accident. But, again, you and your business operations can encourage this. Consider the phrase 'buy one, get one free'. Someone, somewhere, shortened that to BOGO (leaving *free* implied) – and they told two friends, and they told two friends ... Now, people who were not even in on the original shorthand know what that term means if they see it in an ad or hear it from a retail clerk.

Clerks and other front-line personnel are ideally situated to bring this lingo to the masses. Just using proprietary words and phrases among themselves, where they can be overheard on the floor or at the front desk, piques the interest of listeners. You can also ask these employees to 'translate' for customers. By broadcasting your unique language, front-line employees advance the company's brand and solidify it in the minds of customers.

One company that does this doggedly is the women's clothing chain Chico's. They have an ingenious method of engaging even the most casual of window shoppers: upon entering the store, clerks learn the name of customers and write it on a fitting-room chalkboard. Whether they were planning to buy anything or not, the shoppers' personalized changing rooms await. Now that the customer has been drawn in, they are made privy to the company's secret language: clothing sizes. Their sizing differs from the typical numeric or small–medium–large scale; it ranges from 000 to 4.5. Of course, the sizes correspond to conventional sizes – but that's not immediately apparent. Customers must ask a salesperson to 'translate', or simply try clothes on to see which sizes fit.

The classic manner in which unique buzzwords or phrases are delivered to the public, however, is through advertising. I'll leave it up to your marketing team and the creative minds at your advertising agency to devise the right slogan. The upshot is, when the public hears those words, an image of your company comes to mind. If you have done your homework, that image will project your organization's unique culture.

Pillar V review

What are some positive results of developing a unique workplace culture?

Shared experiences and attitudes bring employees together. A cohesive team forms a welcoming environment, which attracts the best talent and encourages them to stay. This brings down costs and builds effective teams that advance company objectives, all of which show in improved revenues.

How is brand uniqueness identified?

Companies can gauge their uniqueness by identifying their products' or services' unique selling points – the elements that differentiate them from the marketplace competition. Selecting and defining a particular target clientele can also help businesses to set themselves apart.

How can a unique company vocabulary promote good culture?

Speaking the same language fosters teamwork and personal closeness among co-workers. This both builds and extends trust, in individuals and in the company itself. As trust grows internally, your clients and customers sense this dynamic and place their trust in you.

Notes

1 Gallup (2017) [accessed 3 June 2017] State of the American workplace [Online] www.gallup.com/file/reports/199961/SOAW%202017%20FINAL.PDF

2 *Chicago Tribune* (2015) [accessed 28 July 2017] McDonald's: 60 years, billions served, *Chicagotribune.com* [Online] http://www.chicagotribune.com/business/chi-mcdonalds-60-years-20150415-story.html

3 Berkus, D and Shepherd, K (2015) *Get Scrappy: Business insights to make your company more agile*, The Berkus Press

Pillar VI: listening

08

Having mentioned how important it is to express the company's vision and operating standards through speech, we must now flip the coin and place the same emphasis on listening. Being a great listener, and having a company filled with purposeful listeners, is the ultimate weapon if you aspire to great culture. If everyone talks at the same time, no one hears. Encouraging tribal speak alone is not the full equation of unique expression; there must be receivers, and give and take.

This creates the sort of open atmosphere that employees thrive in – which attracts great talent and has all those trickle-down benefits for your business that we mentioned in the last chapter. Again, don't let the emphasis on expressing ourselves and disseminating information overshadow the need to listen, and the power it gives our companies: *every person, at every level, in every department raises their value and the effectiveness of the company based on their ability to listen.*

In this chapter, we will take an honest look at how many people fail to listen well, and why that is antithetical to good team communication, business decisions and company culture in general. I will share the common obstacles to the type of meaningful listening that lets us make mental connections and reach clear conclusions, and I will let you know how you can set an example for your team to make the most of their listening skills – and their ability to be heard – in order to better support each other and the company's mission.

How we listen

People talk; we hear what they say and process it. How hard can it be? Hearing, as we know, is not the same as listening, which is not all that easy to do deeply and well. People tend to be overconfident in their exercise of this seemingly simple faculty. But the ability to listen meaningfully is not innate, like hearing. It requires skill that must be sharpened and honed in each interaction and conversation we have, particularly at the professional level.

Many years ago, I was invited to participate in a high-level CEO group. Although similar to Vistage, an international group in which leaders share industry and problem-solving information, this group operated more intensely, on a more personal level. In my first year as a member, I felt like a young schoolboy being tossed into a university class. I didn't know the lingo, my experience level was well behind the average, and my thoughts were tactical and not strategic enough. I knew I was in over my head.

Yet, it was exactly the kind of training ground I needed in order to test new ideas and expand my knowledge. Over that first year I began to notice some patterns about the members I admired most, masters who steadily built on success over the course of their careers. The best of the best in that room of CEOs were open, honest, welcoming of new ideas and change, and – most importantly – they were great listeners. It was not uncommon for them to sit quietly, eyes and ears trained on what other members were saying. They might take notes or ask for clarification occasionally, but they were highly focused on each member as they spoke. It was rare to see them on their phone, computer, or doing anything else that might divert their attention from the conversation.

This stood in stark contrast to others who seemed always distracted, talked constantly, inserted their opinions repetitively, and revealed their failure to grasp the true, underlying factors of the issue at hand. The best listeners hardly spoke, but when they did, it was impactful. In my head, I began referring to these members as listening ninjas. They exhibited a discipline and training that I did not. They saw right through the most complex issues with razor-sharp clarity. How, I wondered, did they do it?

'We have two ears and one mouth so that we can listen twice as much as we speak.' Remembering this old saying by the Greek philosopher Epictetus, I sought to emulate my role models. I noticed that the amount of time they spent listening versus talking was huge, at about a 10 to 1 ratio. Most people get that backwards and talk too much. Imagine listening 10 times as much as you speak, especially in a lively conversation with peers!

In watching these masters of business, I realized that listening was critical to their success, and doing it well set a noteworthy example inside their organizations. In other words, it positively affected company culture. I was excited to find another way to influence my staff as a group, so I made improving this skill a priority for myself.

First, I had to consider where I fell short of the ideal. Although I have always been very good at getting the gist of situations and quickly understanding what the problem or point might be, I was still missing perspective because I failed to listen well or to persist in it. The poorer listeners in our group shared a tendency to click off too early, I had noticed, myself included. So, I learnt that good listening requires a greater measure of self-discipline and long-term focus.

There is far more to listening then just waiting to insert your opinion during a break in the conversation. Business author Stephen Covey sums this up perfectly: 'Most people do not listen with the intent to understand; they listen with the intent to reply.'[1] When I read this quote again with fresh eyes, I knew I had so much to learn. He had described my listening style.

I started to 'watch' myself listen. As I heard things, I mentally grouped them by whether or not I could reply to add value or comprehension to the topic. Instead, I should have been listening to find new information, deeper truths, or details I didn't already know. I don't need to try to be the smartest person in the room.

So, what are the marks that we should be hitting to get the most out of what our colleagues are saying? Perhaps the best way to start talking about that is to identify what gets in the way of effective listening. Major barriers include:

- external distractions;
- internal distractions;
- cognitive biases.

These obstacles are so pervasive that we must consciously acknowledge them before we can move on to actually improving our listening skills. Let's raise awareness of these hindrances so we can get to the positive steps that you can take to instil good listening into your company culture.

Barriers to meaningful listening

Consider the physiological side to listening – hearing. What keeps sound from entering our ears clearly enough to make judgements on its value? What takes our attention away from listening to these sounds in order to comprehend their meaning? Background noise, distracting activities and mental diversions are the biggest ones. We will get to the sound barriers in a moment. First, how about those mental blockades?

Back in Chapters 3 and 5, we touched on how cognitive bias distorts our thinking, often preventing us from communicating clearly and analys-ing data objectively. Being transparent in our exchange of information, and measuring often and accurately, will help us to overcome incorrect conclusions or beliefs caused by these biases. We must also circumvent cognitive biases when it comes to listening. After all, what could be a more subjective means of gaining knowledge?

How well we listen, whom we listen to, and what we act on may depend on a vigilant awareness of potential biases, one of which is selective listening. In the continual flow of input, our brains need to filter with lightning speed what to take in and what not to take in, so we often make quick, unconscious decisions. We cannot hear everything and put our full focus into listening to everyone all the time. So, we pick and choose.

For instance, if you are having a management-level meeting for your high-tech company, and several people bring up the difficulty of retaining the youngest people in the workforce beyond six months, you might sit up and take notice. On the other hand, if your neighbour, George, who is a mechanic and has no managerial experience, starts talking to you about retaining young workers, you might not listen. Now, George may have some excellent ideas on this topic. By assuming that he doesn't, you have closed yourself off to potential solutions that could save your company money.

Clearing the way for good habits, then, depends on knowing what you are up against. Let's spell out what causes communication breakdown, in general, and how these things affect your ability to process what you hear. In the next section I will give you some tips on avoiding these pitfalls. Be on guard for these listening disruptors.

External distractions Mobile phones, advertisements, marching bands ... outside disruptors to your hearing and attention come in small, medium and large. To pay attention to a conversation, you may have to ignore the loud hiss of steam from a nearby espresso machine or a heated discussion among co-workers. You might have to overlook visual eye-catchers like flashing lights or talking heads on television. Anything outside of yourself that interrupts your attention span is a killer to thoughtful listening.

These distractions, such as incoming phone calls or co-workers who talk too much, intrude on your focus. Or, you may break that focus in response to external delights, like reading text messages or e-mails, or switching your concentration to what is playing on television or radio programmes. Humans are capable of filtering out distractions, although some may take more effort than others to ignore. As you listen, be aware of things that you can consciously choose *not* to pay attention to.

Internal distractions What goes on inside our bodies and minds can very easily jar us off course when attempting to listen. Physical symptoms of hunger, fatigue or pain take our minds off what our bodies consider less pressing needs. Boredom, worry and having a very full schedule can do the same. All of these things may affect either the speaker or the listener, or both.

Suppose you didn't sleep well last night and have not had the eye-opening benefit of a caffeinated drink or trip to the gym. Or, maybe your meeting partner skipped lunch and cannot put together a coherent sentence as a result. Being aware that physical or mental concerns might throw you off track can help you minimize your focus on them.

Cognitive biases You will recall many of the mental and emotional things that cloud our perceptions from previous chapters, such as:

- holding a fixed mindset about beliefs or potential outcomes;
- making inferences based on scant information;
- misreading body language or other cues to someone's state of mind;
- casting greater importance on recent versus past events.

These things directly affect our *will* – rather than our ability – to listen. To them, I would add emotional judgement calls based on whether or not you actually like the speaker or respect their intellect. More on how to discount these disruptors in a moment. Let's look at another way in which our brains are wired to distract us with thinking 'short cuts'.

Regressive thinking

I broadened my quest to become a better listener, which was grounded mainly in subjective experience, by gaining some scientific perspective. For this, I turned to a favourite book by my friend and mentor Mark Goulston, MD: *Just Listen, Discover the secrets to getting through to absolutely anyone.* His insights come from 30 years as a crisis psychiatrist, which he also applied to work as an FBI hostage negotiation trainer and assistant clinical professor of psychiatry at UCLA. His theories into the evolution of the human brain shed light on why we communicate the way we do – and how we can avoid some of the barriers that our own cognitive styles create.

Mark Goulston joined me on my radio show, TalentTalk, a few years back, and we spoke at length about listening and how our abilities are linked to brain evolution.[2] Over millions of years, he recounts, the brain has developed into three connected parts, often described as the reptile, mammal and primate layers. Despite their convergence, they work at odds with each other as external situations change. The one that negatively affects our communication skills is the lower reptilian brain, which controls our fight-or-flight response, once our most important survival instinct. Although no longer crucial, this trigger persists when we feel threatened. It pushes aside all other thoughts and desires.

This thought pattern impairs our ability to listen clearly when some measure of fear arises, whether of life-threatening consequence or not. When this part of the brain takes over and a person decides they must fight or run away, having a meaningful conversation is nearly impossible. Discourse is much better enabled by our other cognitive drivers, the mammal and primate sections of our brains.

The middle, mammal section of brain hosts your emotions. This is where the most intense of your feelings hang out, such as joy, love, anger and grief. Finally, the third, primate area of the brain is your rational or logical centre. This is where practical decision making takes place, based on all the input and stimuli you receive.[3]

Goulston has spent his career helping people refine their thinking towards a less instinctual and more rational expression by moving from the reptile brain to the mammal brain, and then into the primate brain. In hostage negotiation, for example, he knows that people cannot listen, or be listened to, when they are controlled by fear, anger or grief, so he can work to undo those strictures. We can apply his techniques to everyday business situations.

Client relations or internal company interactions may depend on circumventing reptilian thinking. The salesperson offering an automation solution to a person whose job it might replace is a classic example. We must project how our actions will affect those on the receiving end. To do so, we must be good listeners. This can be difficult when someone is upset with us. Finding a way to hear what they are saying, while not reacting to their anger or disappointment and engaging our own fight-or-flight response, takes practice and awareness. Acknowledging the barriers we face is the first step towards communicating in a way that allows both parties to utilize more evolved thinking, and to reach better decisions.

Better listening

Putting listening into the context of corporate culture requires focus on the individual audience in a conversation – you, the listener – and opportunities and support for your staff to listen well and to be heard. I introduced some of these in our look at communication channels in Chapter 4. Now, let's break down the skill set needed to get better at the practice of good listening yourself, and how to model and create ways for the rest of your team to incorporate it. Together, these efforts will help you to prop another pillar beneath your growing company culture.

Become a better listener

I hope you have already made a commitment to improving and showing others your listening skills. Like me, you will need to evaluate where you are weak and get new ideas for how to become stronger. Most people struggling to be better listeners have one or two key areas where they fail. See which of these five standards for deeper listening you meet, and which ones you can add to your repertoire.

Listen to understand, not to reply

Take Stephen Covey's advice and move your desire to reply to a lower priority than your desire to learn and understand. Often, people are afraid to let silence or a moment of contemplation occur once their conversation partner stops speaking. In an attempt to look smart or attentive, we feel a false pressure to interject or respond immediately.

Don't worry; you can decide *whether* to respond when the other person has finished talking. Take notes if you need help remembering key points or topics. Remember to be patient. The current moment may not be your final chance to give input.

When you really get into the zone of this process, a few things start to happen. First, you will enjoy a deeper understanding of what the other person is saying. Second, the other person will feel they have been heard. The listening masters in my life all seem perfectly calm as they take the time they need to deliberate about what they just heard. It is powerful to watch.

Repeat back what you heard

This is the equivalent to internalizing facts by writing them down, as you would when taking notes in science class. Unless you have a photographic memory, you need repetition to solidify what you hear in your mind. Particularly when discussion topics are complicated or emotional, take a moment before responding – if you are going to reply – to recap a summary of what you heard. This displays your attention and wish to avoid misunderstanding.

When you do this, your partner might remind you of a detail that you forgot, or one they forgot to mention. Thank them for any clarifications, or apologize if you missed something significant. This two-way listening 'insurance' builds camaraderie and trust, two vital elements of good company culture.

Manage your time

Set a fixed amount of time for meetings or, more casually, to hear someone's views. It is easy to stop listening if we are anticipating what we will be doing next. When you designate time parameters, you are free to relax, focus on discourse, and not worry about other pressing items.

Minimize distractions

No matter how common or necessary multitasking might be, meetings and conversations are not the settings for more than one focal point. If you know you will need to take a call or break away, announce this beforehand. Otherwise, turn off mobile phones and other electronic distractors. If you are meeting in a public place, seat yourself away from the coffee machine or television.

You can plan ahead in order to prevent internal distractions from interrupting your train of thought and discourse. Fuel up before a meeting that might delay your lunch. Get some extra sleep before a co-worker's big presentation. Make a conscious effort to put your worries or daily schedule aside for the amount of time that you have allotted for listening. Schedule meetings when participants will be at their most attentive, rather than at the end of the day, when everyone is thinking about going home.

Prepare to focus

Even with all of your best efforts, your mental state will largely dictate how well you pay attention. You can incorporate periodic stress – relief practices that benefit both of those things. Consider meditation or other mindful practices or scheduled breaks in the day to allow your brain to reset and calm down. These do not have to take place during work time to be effective.

Meditation is becoming more and more popular among entrepreneurs looking to get ahead, who use it for everything from decreasing daily stress to increasing positive energy before speaking engagements. The online news outlet *Business Insider* rounded up a list of 14 top corporate leaders who credit meditation for much of their success.[4] Business moves fast. The brain needs time to get caught up, slow down, and restore harmony. If you get overwhelmed as the day goes on, and find it harder and harder to listen, regularly practising meditation, yoga or an engrossing sport or hobby may solve that problem.

Help people to hear and be heard

Being heard is often an integral part of an overall negotiation. One of my favourite negotiation books is *Start with No,*[5] which introduces the concept of 'three plus'. This approach suggests repeating information at least three times, in different ways, if possible, to raise the likelihood of it being heard and processed. Not being heard is often as simple as someone not remembering, or the information not sticking the first time they hear it. If you have a few specific things the other party really needs to hear, say it more than once.

Another theme from Camp's book is creating the space to be 'un-okay' with a topic. In situations in which the other person may not want to hear what you have to say, taking a less strident and more subtle approach will work, whereas dominantly asserting authority will likely backfire. You can shift the dynamic by relating an example of a recent failure or mistake you made. Expressing vulnerability and being sincere will help the other person to relax and be more open to listening.

Nurturing the personal dynamic opens ears. If you can formulate your wording to ensure the conversation highlights any benefits for the other person, they are more likely to listen. Starting off the conversation by using the word 'I' and making it all about you, will certainly turn them off.

So, try to illuminate an upside for the listener. At the same time, establish a connection and make it clear that you like or respect the person. If you don't, find a diplomatic neutral ground. By signalling to the other party that you like or respect them – or, at the very least, that you don't dislike or disrespect them – you will encourage them to treat you the same way and listen to what you have to say.

Facilitate better listening

Listening well ensures that others feel heard. A 2017 study published by Quantum Workplace shows that this is vital to employee engagement.[6] They surveyed 500,000 employees across 8,700 organizations and found that the top driver for engagement of nonmanagement (individual contributors) employees, was the belief that they are heard. Well, if people want to be heard, we had better be good listeners.

I don't know of an organization that has more managers than lower-level employees. As we have seen, allowing the rank and file to contribute their voices to the corporate conversation holds some key benefits beyond their level of happiness at work. When true bottom-up communication begins to flow, the best organizations are better able to identify areas of improvement. By knowing what the real obstacle is, they can work towards the right solution.

Another benefit is product enhancement and discovery. The people doing the work often have practical ideas on small changes that can streamline operations. Many companies, like Facebook, Google, 3M and General Motors, sponsor hack-a-thons, or brainstorming/problem-solving sessions devoted to innovation. Other companies just ensure that new ideas and innovations are regular topics of discussion at meetings with direct reports. Either tactic is startlingly revealing. 3M scientists are famous for having accidentally invented an adhesive that was so weak, it worked perfectly for sticking paper to the wall.[7] Employees who started using the 'sticky notes' at work are credited with sending this ground-breaking idea to market as Post-it notes.

Would managers at your company have listened well enough to their direct reports to consider the potential of such a product? Make sure your business has a process in place to ask employees for new ideas and suggestions – and that management has a directive to listen to them. Surveys, reviews, exit interviews and meetings with direct reports are all perfect places to start. Formalizing the process shows that the company values employees' thinking about innovation. Culture booster? You bet.

There are more informal ways to listen. Getting people away from work to have a meal, visit a client, or buddy up at a company or team retreat often inspires new ways of thinking. Kim Shepherd of Decision Toolbox does this well. Once a year, she brings together hundreds of employees from all over the country for a gigantic company meeting. During the event, the staff break up into smaller groups for some focused activities. One of them is an ideal way to facilitate better listening habits. She asks employees, 'If I gave you a million dollars to spend on the company, on anything you want, what would you do with that money?' No doubt, staff members have been sitting on the answer to that, just waiting for a chance to voice their opinions. But their ideas are far more practical than the fantasy question might prompt. Shepherd reports that the company does implement the majority of their suggestions, at very little cost and at noticeable gain for operations. This empowering experience, coming annually and driving day-to-day business practices, lends perpetual motion to Decision Toolbox's culture. What a testament to the power of listening, and of being heard.

Let's not forget the value of those things, in cold, hard cash. If either party is trying to communicate amid the dreaded distractions we have talked about in this chapter, your business loses money. While they compete with distractions for space in their ears and brain, time slips away. If you need another reason to actively facilitate listening, estimate what any five people in your company get paid per hour. Then add all that up, and you will have the total amount spent on a dysfunctional meeting in which people were more concerned with their phones or laptops than the business at hand. Now take that number and multiply it by each mediocre meeting you had in the last week. What a waste.

In recent years, I have seen more and more companies develop some basic rules to manage their in-person meetings. Things like: turn off your devices, give your full attention to the speaker, don't interrupt, and avoid multitasking. Often, all we have to do is to ask everyone in the room for their attention at the outset. They just need that reminder. By giving them feedforward and letting them know in advance that you need their full attention for the duration of the meeting, you establish the right atmosphere for great discourse.

As a wrap-up, here are your tools for opening up the 'ear waves' in your organization for effective listening:

- Identify and curtail distractions.
- Set a time frame for paying attention.
- Request input from staff regularly.
- Act on that input to show that you were listening.
- Call out behaviour that interrupts the comprehension process.
- Model good listening yourself.

Pillar VI review

What are some barriers to effective listening?

Paying attention to mobile phones, working on the computer, or focusing on background noise distracts listeners from the outside.

Internally, being too hungry or sleepy to pay attention can make it difficult to follow a speaker's line of reasoning. Cognitive biases such as fixed mindsets or disliking an individual may prevent listeners from hearing and accepting what others have to say.

How can you become a better listener?

Tricks such as setting a time frame for devoting yourself to paying attention and resisting the urge to respond on reflex help you to be conscious of your listening skills. Repeating aloud the information you just heard helps you to retain it and lets the speaker know you understand.

How can you facilitate others in listening well?

The best way to instil good communication habits in your staff is to model good listening behaviour by not interrupting, replying only when relevant, and showing others that you use to the company's advantage the information that you hear.

Notes

1 Covey, S (1989) *The Seven Habits of Highly Effective People: Powerful lessons in personal change*, Simon & Schuster, New York

2 TalentTalk (2015) [accessed 17 June 2017] Mark Goulston [Online] http://www.talenttalkradio.com/e/mark-goulston-03312015/

3 Goulston, M (2010) *Just Listen: Discover the secret to getting through to absolutely anyone*, AMACON, New York

4 Lockheart, J and Hicken, M [accessed 17 June 2017] 14 Executives who swear by meditation, *Businessinsider.com* [Online] http://www.businessinsider.com/ceos-who-meditate-2012-5?op=1/#lesforcecoms-marc-benioff-started-to-meditate-because-his-job-at-oracle-was-so-stressful-2

5 Camp, J (2002) *Start With No: The negotiating tools that the pros don't want you to know*, Crown Business, New York

6 Laubenthal, C and Harris, D (2017) [accessed 19 June 2017] 2017 Employee engagement trends, *Quantumworkplace.com* [Online] https://marketing.quantumworkplace.com/hubfs/Website/Resources/PDFs/2017-Employee-Engagement-Trends.pdf

7 3M (2017) [accessed 31 July 2017] History Timeline: Post-it® Notes [Online] http://www.post-it.com/3M/en_US/post-it/contact-us/about-us/

Pillar VII: mistakes

09

Of all the pillars I have discussed so far in this book, the significance of how companies handle mistakes is, perhaps, the most perplexing concept for executives to grasp. No one stays on top of the game every day. Learning from failure can spell the difference between rebounding and folding.

Without a doubt, the greatest companies know how to do this in a positive way. They capitalize on failure – recall 3M's 'mistake' in inventing Post-it notes from a poor adhesive product. The move from failure to opportunity can occur when company leaders acknowledge their employees' attempts at innovation, rather than just the actual outcomes. Give them a chance to explore, and the right talent will succeed often enough to be effective in their jobs. HR gurus have embraced this idea; you will hear them at conferences again and again, repeating the theme that it is okay for your people to fail.

The problem with mistakes is, it depends. I reserved this pillar of success until last because, as you embark on your cultural quest, you must get this concept right at every level of the business – from the top down. How do you, yourself, accept making mistakes? Leaders must set the example here, demonstrating not irritation but a willingness to learn from mistakes. Then they should tolerate this balance in staff members at every level of the company. It does no good to allow management the freedom to fail while punishing the entry-level employee. The reverse is true as well: we cannot ask entry-level and middle-management staff to learn and move on when they don't succeed, but punish senior management for taking a calculated risk that fails.

Accepting and expecting to grow from wrong decisions or poor outcomes is a hallmark of good culture, and the final one that you will need to become familiar with in order to run a well-rounded business. In this chapter, we will discuss the spectrum of mistakes, from minor errors to epic failure. Never fear, however; I will relay what I know about how making mistakes on the job leads to improvement and even colossal business success. Of course, there is a time and place to mend fences, so we will also look into ways that mistakes can be corrected or overcome.

What are mistakes in business?

You cannot create a policy for dealing with mishaps and misfortune without defining what success and failure look like in your company. After you do that, you must decide how to inform your employees of your attitude towards both. Will there be big bonuses for big wins? Grave consequences for missing the mark? You will be more likely to take a middle-of-the-road approach and place an emphasis on job performance once you realize the value of mistakes.

Of course, you don't want to elevate thoughtless errors to the realm of culture-building experiences. So, let's remove those from the definition by, first, considering the difference between mistakes and errors.

Accept mistakes, not errors

When we think about mistakes, it is easy to dive right into a long list of errors. I have asked groups of conference attendees to shout out mistakes in their company, and nine times out of ten, they list errors. So, what is an error? For our purposes, the definition is fairly cut-and-dried: an error in business context is something simple that you did wrong, which should have been right.

Errors occur when we miscalculate figures, don't check our work, or go too fast and miss details. Anyone should be able to objectively recognize an error in performance that deviates from a clear, correct way to achieve a desired outcome. In other words, Jane didn't follow procedure; she failed to achieve the objective. A good example of this is payroll. If you are a payroll clerk and in charge of calculating hours or entering monetary figures, and you do one of those things wrong, that is an error. Should that happen once, it is forgivable, but if you keep messing up the payroll, you will not have a job for very long.

To be clear, I am not asking you to tolerate a person who is careless with their work and fails to ensure accuracy. We can help that person with retraining, support and even technology. But, if they cannot get it right consistently, we are better off finding someone who can. Another example of an error, though, might have occurred with the bad hire in the first place. If you have a manager who consistently selects people who do not perform or stay with the company more than a few months, this is a serial error. You either have to help them with training and support from other managers and HR, or stop letting them hire people.

Errors come from carelessness, overwork, multitasking and asking people to do work they are not inherently suited to do. That is a loaded sentence, so let's break it down:

Carelessness These errors happen when we fail to care about the outcome or the people who might be impacted, as when a receptionist disconnects callers during a busy spell. This sort of behaviour can stem from incompetence or passive-aggressive 'grudge' motives for choosing not to care enough about what they are doing.

Overwork We see errors caused by this circumstance all the time. When people work too many hours or too many shifts, they become mentally or physically overwhelmed and lose the ability to catch simple errors. While not intentional, the poor or accidental outcomes are often costly.

Giving the wrong medication to a patient, forgetting equipment on a job site or missing key issues in a safety checklist are grave errors with a direct causal influence. People need enough time to rest and recharge, or errors will happen. This is why truck drivers' hours on and off the road are so closely dictated.

Multitasking The idea that we can do many things at once, and do them well, is one of my favourite myths to unmask. Multitasking does not work. In fact, we do less work, with more errors, when we try to do many things at once. Have you ever been in a meeting when the person speaking gets a text message and tries to surreptitiously read it? They try to keep talking, while trying to read the phone display and process the message. They slowly stop talking, finish reading the message and then attempt to come back to the conversation. They don't remember where they left off. They didn't hear any of the responses and will not remember much about the message they just read.

The world is asking us to multitask all the time. The ease of using our mobile phones tricks us into believing this is possible. But, errors happen when we shift our focus and try to keep another process going at the same time.

A Michigan State University study found that interruptions of 3.0 seconds or less doubled errors, while interruptions of 4.4 seconds or more tripled them.[1] Think about those times when driving a car and you get lost, or the visibility is bad and you need to focus. What do you do? You turn down the radio, of course, or tell everyone in the car to be quiet. Our brains need to focus, without interruptions, especially in tasks with a high probability of error.

Low aptitude Errors are also likely if you have a person doing a job for which they are not equipped. Lack of adequate skill, training or passion for a particular position results in a poor fit, which will always bring errors into the workplace.

In running my business, I learned the hard way about this phenomenon. So often, employees or friends would suggest I hire someone they knew because that person really needed a job. If I had an opening, and the candidates were struggling to pay their bills or feed their kids, I gladly gave them a shot.

Unfortunately, in most cases, this was a disaster. I didn't hire them because they had the skills or experience to do the job. They did not take the job because they had a passion for its duties or my business. The job was given out of charity and taken out of desperation. Typically, error upon error occurred, despite our best intentions, and both parties wound up in a tough spot. When this happens now, I avoid my error by consulting my network and introducing those in need to colleagues with job openings that will be a good fit.

Identify real mistakes

One of my most memorable mistakes occurred not at work, but when I agreed to buy my daughter a pet pig for her birthday. Note that I live in the suburbs, and not on a farm or property that is made for pig habitat. Therefore, this pig was meant to be a part of the family and live as much indoors as it would outdoors. It would not have been my first choice, but it seemed like a workable idea. I thought we could manage any pig-related obstacles that came along.

We did some research about keeping pigs as pets and found some nice people selling a piglet. They had quite a menagerie, and I noticed that all their pigs, dogs and cats seemed to live in harmony. We took our little guy home, and my daughter was ecstatic. As planned, for a few days we kept our large mastiff/boxer dogs separated from the pig. Then we slowly tried to introduce them.

This did not go well. The dogs didn't like the new restrictions. Then, when set free, they tried to eat the pig. When we rescued it, they started attacking each other. After a few expensive visits to the vet for them and to the doctor to treat a large gash on my own hand, the situation was not getting better. It was getting worse.

I won't tell you how it all ended, but you can guess. Suffice it to say that my dogs and that pig were not meant to be together. But, you can also bet that I learned from that mistake.

This tale illustrates my definition of a mistake: an action motivated by good intentions, undertaken after careful research and in light of positive indications of success – but that still goes wrong. If we wish to promote good company culture, we must deal with such failings quickly and openly.

Follow mistakes towards improvement

Martial arts film star Bruce Lee once expressed a sentiment that should resonate through your workplace culture: 'Mistakes are always forgivable, if one has the courage to admit them.'[2] This is the caveat with accepting mistakes; to receive acceptance, one must take responsibility for having made them – and then endeavour to learn something from them that will either negate or minimize the damage done, or prevent a similar mishap in the future.

When we do these things in a business situation, we avoid compounding losses. But something else happens. We feel free to take calculated risks, and sometimes these pay off spectacularly.

Companies that accept the trade-off – occasional mistakes in the pursuit of progress – are the ones that break new ground or otherwise excel. The prevailing culture supports bold or experimental thinking, which in turn help to define that culture. Can your organization be a place where employees' best intentions and judgement earn acceptance of their mistakes? Can you allow dreamers to dream big and, ultimately, make your business better?

With all the cynics and emphasis on winning in society, this is a hard sell in many corporations. We also have this drive to ensure people are accountable when something goes wrong, so there is an entity to blame. When we don't hold people accountable to admit, share and celebrate mistakes, the finger-pointing begins. There is just one problem. Blame does not naturally lead to an improvement in the circumstance.

The popular theory that mistakes can drive innovation did not arise in a vacuum. You will often see entrepreneurs and inventors turning mistakes into new – and profitable – opportunities. This happened to James Dyson, who founded leading home appliance company Dyson in 1987.[3] An inventor looking to improve on existing vacuum cleaner technology, James Dyson claims to have made 5,127 prototypes of the revamped machine before it met his standards. That means he had 5,126 failures in a row.

In his situation, he had the drive and freedom to work on this idea and use what he learnt from each failure to get closer and closer to success. Will *you* learn from his mistakes? In other words, will you accept that trying and failing is a part of achieving new things?

Another champion in the area of innovation and mistakes is 3M. We have already seen how the company turned what they thought was a failed formulation into new, marketable product – those Post-it notes – that today is a must-have in any office. Back in 1948 they had already figured out what most companies still struggle to accept – that periodic setbacks are essential to progress. William L McKnight, one-time 3M chairman of the board, said, 'Management that is destructively critical when mistakes are made kills initiative. And it's essential that we have many people with initiative if we are to continue to grow.'[4]

The company is very serious about growth and progress. It literally tracks mistakes on a searchable spreadsheet, in case that information becomes relevant later to solving another problem. It is no accident that 3M has brought us some indispensable products, including Scotch brand adhesive tape and their most famous mistake, those 'sticky notes'. Because 3M builds some margin of failure into its model for success, it has the attitude needed to develop truly novel products.

Even if your company does not invent things, the same mindset will help you to deal with other types of mistakes you are bound to encounter. Let's put it in a customer service perspective. Suppose you work as a flight attendant for an airline that takes a very dim view of making mistakes, and a passenger in first-class seating drinks too much and starts making others uncomfortable. What should you do?

In the event of a disagreement, your organization is known to back paying customers, not employees. But, at 30,000 feet, you might be the only person available to make the decision. Will you worry more about doing the right thing for all passengers? Or about what management will do if you make the wrong choice?

We cannot have a giant book of every possible situation for employees to reference. Sometimes they need to take risks or use their best judgement to make a customer happy, resolve a dispute or make a situation safer.

I prefer the Southwest Airlines approach to judgement calls. I spoke with Shari Connaway, director of People at Southwest Airlines, on my TalentTalk radio show in November 2016.[5] She said that Southwest openly lets staff and customers know they will stand by their employees 100 per cent – whatever their choices – if the team members believe they are doing what is best for the customer. If an employee is wrong, then the company will go back and retrain them or provide counselling and other assistance. But they stand by them, no punishment and no regret.

This is the main reason why Southwest's customer experience is so different from that of other airlines. The employees are fun and loose. They are accommodating and empowered. Each employee can confidently try to help customers to the best of their judgement, even in unclear situations, because they know their employer has their backs. The result of taking this risk in customer satisfaction has made Southwest a top player in the domestic US flight market.

This demonstrates the potential for positive outcomes from mistakes versus the negative impact of errors. You don't have to put up with recurring errors. Tax returns still need to be done correctly, cars should be put together so they run safely, and banks need to deposit your money into the correct account. But larger initiatives and projects – say, improving the client or employee experience or increasing profits – are worth the risk of experimentation in the name of success. Many times, if we fail, we can fix it.

How to handle mistakes

Injecting a sensible approach to handling mistakes into your company culture is the responsibility of top management, so get your senior managers on board with this. If they do not go out of their way to own and manage their mistakes, your staff will never follow. Since you are reading this book, start with yourself and make this a priority. Then move it down the line, until every staff member understands company policy in this area. The goal is to get everyone to accept this practice, understand its value, and know that they have the backing from their boss and the company at large.

For organizations that are relatively flat or small, this should take no time at all. If your company is a worldwide brand with tens of thousands of employees, though, you will have to take a two-pronged approach. First, begin doing what I just described in an internal and private way. Second, you will have to demonstrate this through your brand and leverage some good PR so that your clients and employees can see your commitment. Interesting way to build culture on a wide scale, isn't it?

But, how can we apply this approach? We will need to analyse a mistake. Let's start with a few examples and work our way to outlining some simple strategies for everyday responses to unwelcome outcomes.

Here we turn to Zappos, the online shoe and apparel company. A 2010 article in *Fast Company* magazine detailed an epic blunder that cost Zappos $1.6 million in one day.[6] Somehow, the price on every item on their website was set to be no higher than $50. It may have been due to a bad line of code, a bad calculation or – who knows? This may have been a preventable error. To be fair, I was unable to determine whether this was an error or a mistake.

But what is important to our immediate discussion is how Zappos dealt with the loss of more than $1 million.

Despite having language on their website declining responsibility for pricing mistakes, which easily would have allowed them to cancel the orders, Zappos management decided to honour them all. The thinking was, we made the mistake, not the clients. The company lost the money... and made sure everyone knew about it. They publicly released this statement: 'While we're sure this was a great deal for customers, it was inadvertent, and we took a big loss (over $1.6 million – ouch) selling so many items so far under cost. However, it was our mistake. We will be honouring all purchases that took place on 6pm.com during our mess-up. We apologize to anyone that was confused and/or frustrated during our little hiccup and thank you all for being such great customers.'

Their transparency and decision not to punish purchasers for the company's gross error bolstered Zappos's reputation with existing customers and the general public. But, I wondered, what effect did it have on the employees?

How management handled this issue must reflect how they deal with mistakes internally. Empathy, transparency and fairness all seem to be likely directions. Had they focused on blame, their public statement would ring hollow. Zappos employees know that the company is going to deal with mistakes judiciously and swiftly, all while being generous to their clients (and, we expect, their staff) in the process.

By way of contrast, let's look at a negative approach to mistake management. This happened to me soon after college graduation, when I was working as director of operations at a new hotel in Hollywood, California. The hotel had quickly become popular with movie stars who were shooting films nearby.

One day, one of our regular clients who was getting a low rate in exchange for a long-term stay asked our best front-desk staff member for a favour. He had some friends coming in and wanted them to stay in the room opposite his, and he wanted them to get the same low rate. To do this, the front-desk person had to agree to a rate that she was not technically authorized to approve, and she had to move a prior reservation to free up the room. The discount was not far below our standard rate, and it seemed like a good on-the-fly decision to help a loyal client. Given the exposure the hotel was getting from accommodating this patron, the employee thought she was doing the right thing.

However, when the general manager found out, he was livid. He did not like her approval of the lower rate. Unknown to anyone else, he had booked some of his friends in that room across from the star, as a treat for them – but had kept it a secret. In the end, the front-desk person, a well-loved staff member with much relevant knowledge about the property and the area, was fired.

When our resident celebrity found out, he packed his bags and went to a new hotel. We lost a repeat customer, our best front-desk person and the publicity the movie star had generated, all for a $45-per-night discount. Looking back on this, I would label that disaster a compounded mistake – not by the employee, but by the manager.

This bad example is the kind of knee-jerk reaction to discord that employees complain about all the time. They tell me in trainings and mention it on anonymous surveys, and I hear about the conflicts from HR departments as well. What do these complaints say about the culture at these companies? That it needs work.

There, I have made my case. All of the examples in this chapter highlight the value of 'forgiving' mistakes in exchange for intangible benefits – innovation, better brand reputation and better company culture – all of which often translate to increased revenues or profits. Need I say more?

Handling your company's mistakes

If you don't know where to start in crafting a 'mistake' policy, I'll remind you to start at the top. Here is some advice on how to do that, plus some more tips on moving mistake management into the fabric of your company culture:

Model your policies Get your team together and tell them about one of your failures and how you handled it. Then ask them to join in and share. When I first tried this, the silence among my staff was deafening. So, for months I went out of my way to share my mistakes and what I learnt from them. That broke the ice.

I found that a good way to get people to open up is by gathering in smaller groups. Try this process at the team level. When it comes to revealing sensitive topics in discussion, employees tend to trust people they work closely with more than those in other parts of the organization.

However you do it, removing the veil to show that none of us are perfect is a good first act. Then, simply continue to model the following behaviours and mindsets.

Accentuate the positive Let your staff know that you see the value in learning and growing from mistakes. This encourages big dreams and opens avenues for improvement. Adopt a growth mindset, in which everyone expects to learn and get better a little at a time. Like 3M does, record information gleaned from mistakes in a searchable database for later use. Not all of our mistakes will be turned into new product or practices, but we can retain and recycle the knowledge gained from it.

Appreciate the process Calling a retrospective meeting after a failure lets you celebrate what went right with a project and understand what went wrong. In handling these meetings without casting blame, you will throw the focus on the work process, not mistakes. I am still surprised how much detail people volunteer whenever we do this after the type of Scrum sprint that I mentioned in Chapter 5. A meeting designated just for this purpose lets team members own their mistakes and voice their thoughts on the overall process in a respectful environment.

Accept that 'right' is relative Remember James Dyson, and realize that it may take several (or several thousand) wrongs before you make a right. There is a reason we do A/B testing on websites, market research, surveys and testing. The right answer is out there, and may be changing all the time, so we need a process that is fluid and pliable. Allow your people to try things without asking them to have the correct answer the first time.

Reward, don't punish When we celebrate mistakes and reward people for sharing, documenting and improving on mistakes, we create a forward-thinking trajectory. This is not a crazy suggestion. Intuit, the business and financial software company most famous for their QuickBooks product, is known for celebrating failure.[7] The company sponsors failure parties and gives out awards for the best failures. They use these opportunities to teach, inspire and raise the odds that the next big idea is around the corner.

You can try this by announcing a weekly prize for the biggest mistake. This encourages employees to share their errors, and for the larger team to observe and want to join in doing so. Here, we are rewarding people for the courage to admit mistakes, not for doing the wrong thing. Quite the opposite – any new intelligence gained may help the company down the road.

Choose transparency Let your public relations team talk about company missteps; tell your clients in a newsletter; let your sales team show how they deal with mistakes. A public stand not only demonstrates your commitment to improvement, but weaves a tighter cultural fabric for everyone. Remember Zappos's $1.6 million loss? Who knows how much the company gained from it?

Transparency with mistakes can also be a fantastic place to document or log these occurrences. This is not to punish or embarrass anyone, but instead a way to shed light on the issues and solutions for future employees to review. Companies have created large databases of mistakes, used their own employees' mistakes as training manual examples, and created training exercises to ensure the best of the experience is remembered, and the worst is not repeated.

Make this policy a deal breaker You will accept the occasional mistake, as long as those involved take responsibility for doing it. That's all – just don't cover it up or pass the buck. These actions remove the chance to learn. If you have people who cannot or will not share their mistakes, and continue to hide, dodge, blame or avoid, at some point you will have to let them go. These types are a drain on the company culture that you have so carefully built and that will carry your company to success.

Pillar VII review

Why should companies accept mistakes but not errors?

Honest mistakes happen despite someone's best intentions and judgement, and often lead to corporate benefits that might not otherwise have occurred. Errors show careless practices that typically violate correct procedures and have few positive consequences.

What type of improvements emerge from mistakes?

As evidenced by the team input in project retrospectives, individuals who are comfortable facing mistakes can find opportunities in what went wrong for new techniques or solutions.

What is the most important way to show employees that making mistakes is okay?

Admit your own failures, but show how they offer ways to learn and innovate. Make sure that all senior management do the same.

Notes

1 Altmann E (2013) [accessed 1 July 2017] Brief interruptions spawn errors, *Mustoday.com* [Online] http://msutoday.msu.edu/news/2013/brief-interruptions-spawn-errors/

2 SuccessStory (2017) [accessed 31 July 2017] Bruce Lee quotes [Online] https://successstory.com/quote/bruce-lee

3 Mochari, I (2014) [accessed 31 July 2017] Try, try again: Lessons from James Dyson's invention of the vacuum, *Inc.com* [Online] https://www.inc.com/ilan-mochari/vacuum-innovation.html

4 3M (2017) [accessed 15 July 2017] McKnight principles [Online] https://solutions.3m.com/wps/portal/3M/en_US/3M-Company/Information/Resources/History/?PC_Z7_RJH9U52300V200IP896S2Q3223000000_assetId=1319210372704

5 TalentTalk (2016) [accessed 29 April 2017] Robin Schooling and Shari Conaway [Online] http://www.talenttalkradio.com/e/robin-schooling-and-shari-conaway-11292016/

6 Nosowitz, D (2010) [accessed 15 July 2017] Zappos loses $1.6 million in six-hour pricing screw-up, *Fastcompany.com* [Online] https://www.fastcompany.com/1651302/zappos-loses-16-million-six-hour-pricing-screw

7 Stewart, H (2015) [accessed 1 August 217] 8 Companies that celebrate mistakes, *Learningprofessionalnetwork.com* [Online] http://learningprofessionalnetwork.com/8-companies-that-celebrate-mistakes-by-henry-stewart

PART THREE
Culture in action

Engaging the decision makers   10

If Part 2 of this book gave you the tools and materials to build great culture in your organization, consider Part 3 to be the construction manual. Investing in this do-it-yourself project will yield many concrete results, plus an unseen bonus: opening new internal communication channels for delivering your company's unfolding story. This also affects how news travels between the C-suite, HR, and the rank and file. That is what the next two chapters will reveal – how to take what you have picked up here and put it where it will do the most good.

But don't just take my word for it. These touch points were shared with me by people up and down that chain of command. When I first set out to write this book, my goals were to reflect accuracy in my conclusions and to deliver the information to you in a practical style, so that you could use it immediately. So, I set out to test the material on audiences, in person.

As a natural extension of my in-office passion for the topic, I began speaking publicly about company culture. I wondered what the response would be. To my surprise, each conference I spoke at led to invitations to three or four more. This told me my discoveries were resonating with business owners and HR professionals. Although I was happy that my talks were well received, a theme emerged during Q&A sessions and late-night conversations that suggested I had more work to do. I would hear, over and over again, something like, 'Chris, this advice is just what my company needs. But, how do I get my bosses to do this? How do I convince them that this is important, or to realize we have a problem in the first place? They think everything is fine.'

These sentiments are valid. I realized that *my* story about company culture was missing something: how to deliver the message to key players so that its value went unquestioned.

The disconnect between HR and upper management on issues of culture can be vast. HR staff may be focused on attracting talent and mitigating risk, while managers prefer to contemplate novel products and services, and a solid bottom line. In this chapter, we take a look at the avenues between these two groups that serve as the delivery system for new cultural components. Where does that leave employees? I have saved the best for last. It will be up to these people, in the end, to achieve the steps in your company's evolution. We will tackle how to take this remaining group, your staff, to the next cultural level, in Chapter 11.

Review your pillars

You may only get one shot at pitching the power of culture to **the powers that be** (TPTB) – whoever it is in your company that will make the decision to embrace it and set the plan into action. Whether you are a founder, CEO, department manager or HR professional, you will need to convince *someone* in your organization to team up with you and build on your company's culture. This effort will permeate your entire staff hierarchy and procedural operations. It's big – and you will need help from the right people. So, gather all your ammunition first. Here is a quick recap of the seven pillars of success:

- **Transparency** is already embraced by forward-thinking institutions for its role in promoting employee and public confidence in businesses. Open and honest communication and access to information are the bedrock of team cohesiveness and morale. Money saved and generated by greater talent retention and stronger work performance flows directly to the company's bottom line.

- **Positivity** mindsets put companies ahead of the game by making the approach to problems proactive, instead of retroactive. Looking at what is going well allows businesses to capitalize on strengths and not be forced into continually reacting to changing circumstances. It is the ultimate way to improve – by rewiring people's thinking and looking to the future.

- **Measurement** and analysis systems ensure that businesses act on objective information as often as possible. This is another way to stay ahead of the curve and form policy proactively. It also gives you a window into your employees' work experience and, therefore, mirrors your existing culture.

- **Acknowledgement** is the reward that overshadows salaries and benefits for your team's dedication and service. More than just a bonus programme, recognition in various forms fills a basic human need and motivates employees to carry out their day-to-day efforts on your company's behalf. When their commitment is acknowledged, they are more likely to stay with the company and do their best work.

- **Uniqueness** in individual employees reverberates in your company's brand. You should be able to easily identify and articulate what sets apart your people and operation. These unique cultural markers are what sell your products and services, and attract and retain the best talent for the job at hand.

- **Listening** skills lie at the heart of how a company actualizes its mission and vision. Promoting meaningful listening in your organization will lead to more effective teamwork and customer service and, possibly, breakthrough insights that affect business performance.

- **Mistakes** in companies with great culture are not indelible blemishes but opportunities for growth and learning. You can present evidence that rewarding rather than punishing mistakes is a team builder and springboard for innovation. People want to work for companies that accept their human limitations, and they will be quick to move past temporary setbacks towards improvement.

The potential embodied by each of these pillars should be enough to pique the interest of company leaders looking for a next-level shift in performance. Take the tools and materials from each of the pillar presentations in Part 2 of this book to the powers that be (TPTB), and show them that you are ready to set the cornerstone for a structure that will allow your organization to achieve new heights.

Assess company needs

Now is the time to customize what you have learnt here for potential application to your particular situation. Suppose you are connected with that very unique pencil-making company, XYZ, Inc. Which do you think would be the more effective argument: tossing this book on a manager's desk, or describing in detail how culture building will affect XYZ's market share? Let's take the custom approach. First, we will talk about what unique needs or concerns your company can address with a cultural upgrade. Then, in the next section, I'll help you gear your pitch specifically to your CEO or the individuals who will be responsible for accepting or rejecting your ideas.

So, how can you cut through the everyday tasks, problems and noise to grab the attention of the powers that be? By thinking about what your company needs – and what it has to gain from strengthening its culture – in the short and long terms. Where can you make the biggest impact in your operations and outcomes? It could be product development, leadership development, revenue development or vertical growth. You are the one on the inside, and you are the one who realized that the concepts in this book can bring about big positive changes. You must decide what is your company's overriding concern.

Let's say, after several sleepless nights, that you have done this. You have found your *why* for proposing a cultural revolution. Now, how will you frame that? You will need to explain how the seven pillars will address your company's biggest concern. This can go one of two ways – are you looking to mend an otherwise solid structure? Or do you want to start fresh, and transform a loosely connected group of workers into a like-minded team with a common purpose?

Aspirin or vitamin?

Again, let's assume you have answered that question. All that is left for you to do is decide on your delivery system. In the interest of creating a healthy culture that will feed your organization, you must sell your solution as either an aspirin, to soothe specific aches – or a vitamin, to nurture the overall 'body'.

Look at it this way. When we want to take care of ourselves so we will be healthy in the future, we often take a vitamin each day. It is part of an overall strategy to reach our full potential. And yet, a vitamin is a luxury. We can live without it (but might not thrive without it). An aspirin, on the other hand, is something we take to address an acute issue. We have a headache, and we don't feel good. Taking an aspirin will bring immediate relief. It is in keeping with this dynamic that HR professionals, or anyone looking to convince TPTB to make positive change, can frame their proposal. Are you asking them to take a vitamin or an aspirin?

In other words, is the cultural change you want to enact going to be a lengthy initiative that is 'good for us' but not mandatory for our immediate comfort or stability? Or, are you suggesting a change that will bring a swift and promising improvement to a large pain point in the organization, department or team? This is incredibly important to determine ahead of time.

The pillars I have described in this book, taken separately, are aspirins. An ailing company may need one, some or all of them. But, applied in total, and in a sequence appropriate to your business, the seven pillars act as megavitamins. They are what to take to grow robust and remain healthy. A new enterprise, a company with new leadership, or an underperforming enterprise should begin a vitamin regimen for life. Your job, in either case, is to help your boss or your managers understand that either prescription can result in real and lasting change – that addressing the underlying issue, culture, will push the company towards peak condition.

You will recall that I have suggested starting with the hardest and biggest problems to enact tangible improvement. Too often we go for the easy win, or the small thing first. Go for the aspirin issues first! Find the areas giving your company a headache and get everyone feeling better. Can you suggest something that is likely to be viewed as a major improvement?

Perhaps as you have been reading you have identified one particular pillar as an area in which your company's performance or outlook is less than stellar. This generally causes organizations a bit of pain, in the form of hard costs, soft costs, loss of talent, failing to attract and hire top talent, customer attrition, cash flow – whatever is of present concern to your company. What you need to do is articulate that pain in the most overwhelming, yet accurate, way... and then present one or more pillars as the solution.

Gather key data

The worst thing you can do is walk into the meeting with a complaint and no evidence to back it up. If you think your company is in trouble because of poor recognition, hiding from mistakes, or little transparency, you will need more than a few lines of this book to convince someone. Amass clear examples of both what your company has recently struggled with, and a few instances of what other companies have done to succeed. Some of the examples I have used to illustrate my points may suffice or point you towards additional references.

For your company's specifics, you might draw from balance sheets, employee or customer surveys, or comparison charts showing changes in performance. If you don't have these, the *lack* of pertinent data can be a weapon. Or, if all else fails, your own first-hand account, perhaps corroborated by others in your organization, of the strengths or weaknesses upon which you must build or repair, might be persuasive.

Whatever you choose, put it in writing. A verbal exchange is easily discounted. A request in writing deserves a response, and data that supports your request lends it more weight. So, don't miss this step. Get your ducks in a row before setting out to make your case.

Discourage band-aid solutions

Besides being prepared to forward your argument, you should be ready to head off any claims against it or lesser solutions that will not do as much good.

If your company has tried and failed to fix the big problem that you have identified, it is likely that more attention will not be the cure. To counter the assertion that a narrow focus on a pain point will do more good than a larger cultural undertaking, go back to some of the other defenses we have discussed. Copy those graphs that show the status quo isn't working. Copy a few articles about companies that overcame that very problem by turning to a cultural solution.

Or, if TPTB like the idea of working on cultural pillars but want a quicker, easier way to do that, be ready to head off suggestions of cosmetic repairs that don't get to the root of things. Many professionals equate company culture with employee perks and retreats. Those are nice, but they are band-aids, and not wholly effective ones at that.

I knew that, but I wanted to see what a sample of senior HR people had to say. I sent a note to 10 colleagues asking them to list some of the things that they had tried and how that worked out for them. Within three minutes, I had more examples than I could include. Here are a few perks and practices meant to nurture company culture that you might have to shoot down as **poor cultural solutions**:

- **Annual reviews**: these are expected communication devices, but often fail to help the employee or the company.

- **Stand-up desks**: only a few people actually want them, and they can cause additional liability claims if they are not ergonomically correct.

- **Employee discount programmes**: some departments continually chase down cut-rate tickets to movie theatres, theme parks, etc, out of proportion to employee interest and participation.

- **Take-your-kids-to-work day**: with its inherent distractions, this is often a completely wasted day for everyone, often with more negative than positive outcomes.

- **Holiday parties**: these are also expected, but frequently are costly and disappointing, doing little to promote company values or appreciation.

- **Ping-pong/table games**: after the novelty wears off, only a few people ever use them, and they take up a lot of space.

- **Wellness programmes**: their impact on culture is questionable, and needs far more investigation by your company. Their benefit for health, productivity and other possible positives is clear. What is not clear is the impact on improving company culture.

Again, you may choose to have any or all of these programmes at your company, and they probably won't hurt. My point is that programmes, parties and special days are not the type of 'pills' you take to ensure cultural greatness. You can counter suggestions of half-measures like this: you would rather spend your energy – and your boss's or manager's time – on methods shown to create real and significant change.

Choose your target

So, who will be on the receiving end of your wise proposal? You have got two groups to muster: the people you know who are already receptive to it, and the ones who will be deciding whether or not to consider the plan.

Allies

A sweeping measure that will affect everyone in your organization will have a bigger impact coming from more supporters. You might want to consider enacting a team for this very purpose. As I know from generating buzz within my own company, once you start talking about this topic, it grows legs. The idea that from healthy culture all good things flow sounds good to people who don't have to take responsibility for it – yet. The more you throw sparks, the more they kindle excitement. It probably will not take long to win over some converts.

In this case, it doesn't matter whether you have the backing of key managers or employees, as long as they are trusted in the company. If you can enlist someone with influence, either with management or with employees, you will greatly strengthen your case. This is actually a good litmus test for where you stand on the subject. If you cannot get someone on board, either your understanding of these concepts is off base, or you need to work on your presentation of the issue and solution.

Want to see how the topic will be received with upper management before going to the top? Schedule a lunch with five key people in your company, and have a casual conversation about the issues or pillars you feel need attention. Don't mention your master plan. If three or four of them demonstrate passion or energy, start laying the groundwork with them. Later, these people can help you in the implementation process. For now, having their stamp of approval, input and advice will prove invaluable as you move closer to that key meeting with the right leader.

Key decision makers

Depending on the size of your business, you have a couple of choices about whom to approach with your grand design for company culture. You can choose the person who will be most directly affected by a cultural fix to a pain point, or you can go straight to the top. They might be one and the same, or you might identify someone else who would be a better strategic bet. Whoever the right person is, make sure they will have a stake in the immediate and overall outcomes.

Although TPTB at any level of leadership should think first and foremost about the company, taking a personal tack is still a good idea. Show this person how improving company culture might impact their job in a positive way. Are they having trouble retaining talent? Are they making budget cuts due to rising hiring expenses? Many of the worst people problems and cost issues become easier to deal with as the culture improves.

Here's an example of how that works. A woman I'll call Linda ran up to me after my talk at a conference and said that 'listening' was her company's top issue. Leaders didn't listen, employees never felt heard, departments didn't communicate. This disconnect delayed product releases and caused everyone to play the blame game. So, I challenged her to find out what her CEO would say was her number-one headache.

Linda did her homework and told me the biggest issue for her company's CEO was decision paralysis. Employees were not making decisions and, instead, waited for someone else to do so, to avoid blame. This made the case for a cultural overhaul. Linda identified the area to be improved, and her CEO articulated the problem within it that needed a solution. Linda can now suggest exploring how to help the team members become better at listening, which in turn will strengthen company culture and remove her CEO's headache.

Deliver the goods

As you evaluate what your company needs, take your audience into account. This is the trickiest part of your delivery system – you must understand what your audience needs mentally and emotionally, and use your proposal to satisfy it. This includes all of the things we talked about in Chapter 3 regarding the most transparent ways to communicate and convey information. You can use any tools at hand to give your argument a boost – insights into personality, what their position entails and which goals they are trying to reach, knowledge of their personal preferences, etc.

For instance, does this person or team want all the details first, or a bullet-point summary? Will they be more interested in working at the department level, or company wide? Remember to make the conversation two-way, and be prepared to ask them relevant questions that play into their perception of current conditions. Given below are a few more tips on how to make your best presentation.

Be specific

What is in it for the company? That is what everyone wants to know. If the benefits are not clearly articulated, plausible and achievable, it will be difficult to gain interest or to get leadership to agree. There must be a clear and desired outcome from whatever you are suggesting. Try to distil it to a couple of sentences, such as your company vision. Your summary should display that the end result will be worth the concerted effort.

The pillars in this book will fundamentally improve a company, but it is ill advised to show up at a meeting and tell everyone they are terrible at listening, and that they should do something about it. Instead, paint a picture of what it would look like if the company was fantastic at listening – how it would impact revenues, work quality and employee motivation. If profits and happiness go up, and costs and turnover go down, those are the areas to highlight.

Also, be ready to describe what will happen if you don't reach your full potential and the project is only partially successful. Lay out why even a limited result makes it a worthy undertaking. Or, devise an alternative plan, in case the best-case scenario is voted down.

Ask, don't tell

As you introduce the topic of culture, engage your audience by asking a few good open-ended questions. Asking *who? what? where? how?* and *when?* allows people to form a vision on their terms.

Some examples could include: what would happen if employees understood more about the company's finances? Or, how could we educate employees about the company finances? This starts a conversation, rather than risking it all on yes or no. This is why you should avoid a closed-ended question such as: can we share the company finances with employees? That is begging for a no, if your current policy is limited to only a few people.

Try to skirt the fixed mindset about a rule that is already in place. Instead, ask how outcomes might improve if the policy were different. Don't assert authority you don't have, or even ask for permission to change things, but instead ask TPTB to explore the possibilities.

Play to your audience

The final hurdle to presenting your case in the right way, at the right time, involves the possible biases that your audience – the powers that be – will struggle with, simply because they are human. We have touched on this material in several chapters, but you can review the basics in Chapter 3. Here are a few cognitive bias principles we haven't discussed yet that you can use to refine your approach:

Use prospect theory to your advantage

When we present to someone who is senior to us, we must remember that people are inherently more worried about losses than gains – particularly company leaders or stakeholders. This 'prospect theory' was first developed by renowned behavioural scientists Daniel Kahneman and Amos Tversky, whose collaboration is described in a fascinating 2016 *New Yorker* article, 'The two friends who changed how we think about how we think'.[1] Prospect theory holds that people prefer certainty and undervalue small probabilities, two biases that can get in the way of presenting an ambiguous topic such as company culture.

On the surface, promoting culture might seem unrelated to stemming or avoiding corporate losses. Those in power prefer what looks like a sure bet, even if it isn't one. In simpler terms, they want to avoid making decisions they will regret. So, they may discount solutions that are likely to work but that don't come with written guarantees. You can work around this possible roadblock by assuming that your audience, TPTB, will naturally avoid regret, if they believe the risk to be high and the reward unlikely or inadequate.

In order to highlight the upside, use your research, data or testimonials to demonstrate what the real cost of *no change* will be. Give them a hypothetical regretful decision, one that is based on inaction. If you don't, you can bet on the status quo.

Or, show them what a win–win situation looks like. Let's again use the example of being transparent with company financials. Most business leaders will decline this type of transparency, saying that the company seems fine and no one else is asking for this. The safe bet is to keep going the way things are. If you can make the case on a grand and convincing level that financial transparency will yield incredible results and eliminate huge problems and costs, then great. If not, you may need to rely on plan B. What can you suggest the company does that has a small cost and a huge upside?

Timing is everything

Be very careful about setting the time of your meeting with TPTB. People tend to be more focused in the morning and able to deal with facts and figures, and more tired and less patient in the afternoon. Kahneman and Tversky relate why this is so in their work on positive decisions and hunger. In the book *Thinking, Fast and Slow*, [2] Daniel Kahneman describes a study they conducted around decisions by parole officers in Israel. Overall, prisoners were given a favourable parole decision 35 per cent of the time. However, when rulings were made just after the deliberators ate a meal, those in favour shot up to 65 per cent. Even more significant, as the judgement time moved closer to the next meal, the percentage dropped down to near zero. Kahneman and Tversky determined that hunger did not make parole board members cranky or negative. Rather, they discovered that reasoning takes a lot of energy. In the majority of cases, the judges said no. So, if they were running on fumes and low on energy, they would default to what they did most of the time.

This is enlightening information. It explains why in the past I was unable to correctly gauge how my boss would react, despite my convincing arguments. It also explains why I always had a better shot first thing in the morning, or at lunch or dinner. Intuitively, I learned that if it was something big and had a lot of moving parts, to sell I had to take my boss out for a meal. I thought for years that it was the act of getting them out of the office that was important. That might have played a role. But now I know it had more to do with hunger. If you can't present your idea over a meal, offer TPTB a fresh-baked treat, popcorn, or a sweetened coffee drink. This is not a bribe, just a way to set yourself up for success and get the best possible answer.

Overcome confirmation bias

The final cognitive glitch relevant to your situation is confirmation bias. You know this one; it occurs when we look for information that supports our way of thinking, and ignores other facts and opinions that do not. We see social media platforms capitalize on this tendency by delivering us content that they think we will 'enjoy'. They are also delivering us information that tells us we are right, which is designed, in some cases, to sell us stuff. The problem with this is the echo chamber that we enter. Hearing only what we want to hear and believe is satisfying – and dangerous. This was why I suggested in Chapter 3 that you designate a 'devil' in your meetings. Asking people to disagree and provide bad news to the group is not what we typically do, but it may hold solutions or opportunities for improvement.

The powers that be at your company are likely to hear facts and opinions that confirm what they already believe. Who does not want to appease the boss? But yours is a hard sell, with benefits that are concrete but not immediately apparent to the listener. Use these strategies to overcome confirmation bias or make it work for you:

Talk about it. Confront the issue by saying something like, 'I'm not just here to tell you what you want to hear, although I think you will like the results we can achieve.'

Be persistent. Repeat, restate or rephrase key information to ensure that people hear it.

Request forbearance. Ask listeners to withhold judgement until they have heard all the data and all of your testimony.

Discuss alternatives. You don't want to be in your own echo chamber, either, so offer some options.

Asking questions is an easy way to derail confirmation bias. Ask in advance what would need to happen or exist for wide-scale change to occur. If TPTB summarize the objective parameters before you start, they will be less likely to accept only their preferred data. Before they can give you an answer, ask them what good things might happen if they said yes. Finally, whatever the outcome, ask your audience what in your proposal was the biggest takeaway. Their response will help you know how you did, and what work you have to do going forward.

Yes, taken together, all this preparation may be a formidable prospect. But consider what is at stake. Convincing leadership of the value of achieving great culture could be your greatest contribution to the organization. So, lay the groundwork, have good data and examples to support your argument, and present your ideas and solutions when the time is right. Once you get the leaders on board, you will be well prepared to spread the message to those who will enact your plan: the staff.

Notes

1 Sunstein, S and Thaler, R (2016) [accessed 29 April 2017] The two friends who changed how we think about how we think [Online] http://www.newyorker.com/books/page-turner/the-two-friends-who-changed-how-we-think-about-how-we-think

2 Kahneman D (2011) *Thinking, Fast and Slow*, Farrar, Straus and Giroux, New York

Achievement 11

The underlying promises of great culture are high employee engagement, brand awareness and – if all goes well – market domination. If you have prevailed in your Chapter 10 prep work and presentation, your company stakeholders have seen the light. Cultivating culture to its full potential brings clear benefits for everyone involved.

Customers, vendors and shareholders will all gain when a company has all seven pillars supporting its goals and dreams. But, this chapter concerns bringing your message of the power of company culture to its achievers – the employees. They make culture what it is, or is not, in every organization. Stakeholders can show the way, inspiring action and purpose to excel. Individual staff members must then carry out the hard work, forging culture as they go along.

Your final job is to encourage employees to be conscious of how company culture unfolds from their attitudes and actions. This is where HR people, or whoever serves to monitor cultural formation, can exert some control over the process: it is largely dependent on trusting the people we choose to hire and retain to put vision into action.

So, while this chapter is about spreading the message to employees, it is written for you – in whatever role you serve in strengthening your workplace's culture. Here, you will find ways to get the word out and engage team members on every level. As we discussed in Chapter 10, in okaying this effort, owners and stakeholders can prepare the company for success. But is up to workers, and those who select them, to accomplish it. The next leg of this journey is for you (or, if you are a leader, the HR professional whom you designate), not a part-timer or delegate. You will need some key people to help you along the way, but this is your mission, and you must be in charge.

Now, go forth, and spread the word about great culture – and trust in your employees to achieve it.

Set group priorities

In the course of this book, I have identified several 'starting points' – places to begin improving or places to begin gathering support for improvement. This is because every business is different. And so, your priorities for your cultural programme will be unique to your company. Flip back through the pillars of success, or look at the list at the start of Part 2. The goal, of course, is to incorporate all of them, eventually. For now, I will repeat my earlier advice: pick the pillar that represents your company's biggest weakness. It will hold the greatest opportunity for improvement.

In fact, why not chart your course by making a list in order of your greatest areas of concern? Write down what your ideal outcome will be from each one. Then you will be able to tackle the biggest issue first, and circle back through the list. You will keep the focus on each distinct pillar until you reach a predetermined level of satisfaction.

To do this, call a huddle between HR and the appropriate level of management. Together, imagine how the company would look and what you expect to happen and see when you are successful with each pillar, or when you complete the structure. What does that look like? How can you measure what has actually happened?

One way to quantify the effort is to tie each phase to the SMART goals that I introduced in Chapter 5, in relation to KPIs. Set specific, measurable, attainable, realistic and time-based criteria, and then project the results that will occur if you are successful. If you discover new and better benchmarks as you progress, and want to update your vision, great. Just be sure to share it and gain approval from the key players in your movement for change.

Once you know what will be addressed, and what success looks like, there are a few important milestones to accomplish. You need to request participation from your workforce, and then set the plan in motion. First, select the lieutenants who will assist you in what will be a continual effort. They will help you to get the word out and interpret its fine points for the uninitiated. These assistants act as couriers, or, as I call them, **champions** of your message. Champions are the most important people you need. This has nothing to do with sports or competition. Here, the word champion refers to someone highly specialized and skilled who has a particular passion for the change you want. That passion needs to be your change initiative.

Finding people who have a true passion and understanding for why the change is important is mandatory. Your champion must be willing to do just about anything to help you make it happen, and exhibit an energy and positivity about that topic. This energy is reminiscent of when people tell you about their favourite band, try to convince you to support a political initiative, or share interest in a hobby. While explaining, potential champions almost glow. If you can find people who feel this way, your ability to enact change will be fundamentally improved. On a side note, if you cannot find anyone with the passion or energy to help you, this is the time to work on your messaging.

Champions are easy to find, if you are willing to put in the effort to find them. Participate with employees in direct meetings, lunches, calls, or in any situations where people feel safe enough to display their true feelings.

Select your messengers

Your champions will absorb your message and help you to move the cultural revolution from theory to practice. You will choose them for their facility in communication and delegation but, most importantly, for the way in which they respond to the mission. It must be with passion. In dealing with any concept that is broad in scope or complex in detail, putting a strong sense of purpose behind it will help you to surmount difficulties. The team feeds off such positivity. Your champions' passion for pillar concepts will drive your change initiative, so choose them wisely.

For instance, if you are starting with Pillar I, transparency, find people who have a true understanding and appreciation of its relation to healthy culture. You might do this through casual lunch conversations, staff surveys, online posts, or in formal meetings on the subject. An in-person approach is particularly helpful here. You know what it's like to speak with enthusiasm on a topic, whether large or small. When someone is passionate about what they are saying, you will hear it in their voice and see it in their eyes. Those are the champions you want on your cultural team.

Try to pull assistance from all levels of the organization before launching your programme. Adding a few employees will make your proposal inclusive – it's not management issuing a directive, but the whole staff inviting everyone to join in. Ground-floor team members will also have new perspectives on how greater transparency, for instance, will help them, other departments, clients and the company at large. This frames the coming change as positive.

People are often suspicious of change; when their livelihood and work life are involved, they may instinctively worry or fix themselves against the unknown. This is why having champions at all organizational levels will help you. The different factions at your workplace will react, in part, based on their colleagues' reactions. They will want to know what everyone else thinks. This is when your champions – who are among the bunch, listening and participating in conversations – will step in to help, and they will be heard, because they are speaking to peers.

This is powerful, and even more so because they are willing volunteers. They are promoting better culture because they believe in it, and they have the data and the context to back up their views. That's convincing stuff.

But, suppose you cannot find people with that degree of energy to help you instil your message. Don't give up. Now is the time to work on *your* messaging. Ensure that you have shared your vision and explained the outcomes accurately. Look back on the presentation advice in Chapter 10 for strategies that will work at this level, and try again.

Present it to the people

Now that your champions are identified, the time has come for you to share what you are trying to do with employees throughout the company. You will do this informally – in groups – and strategically, with individuals, as needed. Next, I will give you some tips on how to prompt adoption and acceptance of your mission by most of your staff. There will be holdouts who are afraid or just plain stubborn. We'll get to them too. Our immediate focus is in clearly and persuasively delivering the message so that most of them are willing to give the programme a try.

At the team level

Initiating this conversation in a small group setting can be helpful. First, if you generate excitement, you will be easily able to identify additional champions. (You can never have too many.) Second, people are more likely to ask questions and have a dialogue in a smaller setting. If you address 200 people in a large hall, you will get different results than if you spoke to smaller groups that could interact. I've found the ideal meeting size to be 10–12 people at most, but organizations with a global workforce may require a different approach.

In any case, we are looking for people to be comfortable and open. One group that exercises that dynamic is the team. If your company uses teams, and most of them can make a meeting, the quality of reactions and dialogue will be better. By this time, you will have already met with their managers, and they should have prepped the team on the subject for you. However you break the news, just avoid the temptation to get everyone in the room, all at the same time, especially at the start. Small groups allow you to refine your message, deal with objections in advance, and use stories or other data as evidence.

Employ the rule of good timing that I mentioned in Chapter 10, based on Kahneman and Tversky's correlation between hunger and judgements. You don't want the people with a negative bias to fall back on their 'default' answer. You want everyone on board. Plan your meetings for just after lunchtime, or offer refreshments. Again, it's not a bribe, it's an insurance measure.

In the same vein, making people feel welcome and comfortable will set a receptive tone. Avoid stirring up interpersonal drama, cliques or known 'people issues' when deciding who to group together for meetings. Choose a pleasant setting, adjust the air temperature and remove distractions. As with hunger, discomfort tends to overshadow other concerns. If people in your employee audience are too hot, too cold, cannot hear, or are otherwise distracted, they will tune things out and will not retain information.

Once you have the room and human dynamics worked out, you must put team members at ease mentally. There are a few ways to do this:

Ask for their help You can tell them why, and tell them how – but in the end, the rank-and-file employees need to know that you need their help. Ask for their opinions. Ask them to help you see what you have missed. Ask them to imagine the ideal results from what you are about to undertake, and *then* set out to achieve them.

Ask them to experiment Instead of asking people to try, or give it a shot, I ask them to help me experiment. This small change in wording has been like magic for me. It implies a shared sense of purpose without blame. It replaces fear of a definite change with a resolution to test something, measure it, and then decide whether it is worthy to pursue.

Ask them how to do it You might know where you want to end up, but asking team members to help articulate what success would look like to them can clarify or expand those horizons. Employees often have far better practical ideas and solutions, once given the inspiration and permission to come up with them. When they propose the changes and agree to try them, you won't have to beg for results. Their ideas are more valuable to them, and accomplishing their goals is rewarding and empowering.

Ask them to be patient Here we can set realistic expectations that trying to make the company better doesn't happen overnight. Let them know that you don't have all the answers. Acknowledge that not every effort will succeed the first time. But, in the attempt, you can determine how things will work. Together, you will consider how the company can get better today and look to make adjustments tomorrow, so that you can enjoy lasting success down the road.

Ask them to be happy when they leave In many meetings, to get to the heart of matters we often need to bicker, argue and challenge each other. In turn, we often leave meetings less than happy. Psychologist and researcher Daniel Kahneman found that a pleasant experience at the end of an unpleasant experience caused people to forget most of the earlier pain and negative feelings.[1] Maybe that is why the dentist always gave me a toy after filling a cavity! You don't have to announce why, but take care to end your meetings on a pleasant note. Discuss something interesting, recognize someone, or hand out sweets before people leave – anything to connect a positive experience with your new initiative.

At the individual level

Do you have that friend who is always first to get the newest phone or gadget, or who loves to try out the latest restaurant or fad? We call these people early adopters. They are drawn to new things, whether proposed by clever marketers or popular opinion. When it comes to technology and culture, I tend to be an early adopter myself. I am not standing in line for a phone, but I usually get the newest model within a few weeks of its release. Most people take the middle ground. They move over to the newest thing once they can afford it and notice that the earliest adopters are happy.

The last group are the slow adopters. They don't switch phones or anything else until they are forced to do it. Some of my friends have phones that, at any moment, will fall apart. Some may not have the cash or prefer to wait until they truly need a new model. When it is not about money or priorities, though, it is often about change. They don't want to change. They don't want to take a gamble on improvement. They tell themselves that they are happy just the way things are.

You may face a faction of employees who are indifferent to the prospect of better times simply because they prefer the status quo. Your job is to kindle interest among them, to create the momentum required to enact change and, ultimately, achieve success. Your champions' enthusiasm will help, but the foot-draggers can sap their energy and slow the cultural revolution at the ground floor. Let's look at how to get the remaining people on board, one at a time.

Rather than labelling the slow adopters 'difficult', consider that they actually just don't have the information they need to say yes. It is then necessary for you to determine where they are in their understanding and provide incentives to engage in the project. Here is a handy scale to help:

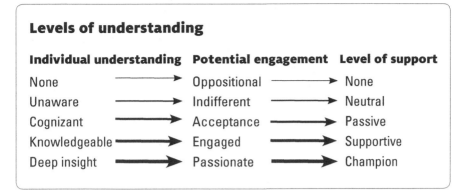

Levels of understanding

Individual understanding	Potential engagement	Level of support
None ⟶	Oppositional ⟶	None
Unaware ⟶	Indifferent ⟶	Neutral
Cognizant ⟶	Acceptance ⟶	Passive
Knowledgeable ⟶	Engaged ⟶	Supportive
Deep insight ⟶	Passionate ⟶	Champion

Determining where someone is in their understanding level is far more effective than trying to convince them to be more engaged because everyone else is. Of course, it is possible for someone to deeply understand and still disagree. I have yet to find that person, when discussing and implementing these pillars, so I cannot address that situation. Instead, let's focus on achieving clarity in the early adoption stages. See if you can identify the holdouts' issues, and then, with their permission, share the information with everyone else. If one person has a question or doubt, others likely do as well.

After group meetings, and then one-on-one meetings, you will have a list of common questions and concerns. You should be able to address them with the data and examples that you have used to win over management and the rest of the workforce. You may end up with a few naysayers who appear to be obstinate but are probably still acting on that old reptilian instinct: fear.

If the fear of change is preventing these folks from taking up the cause, you can try something that worked for me. Back when PeopleG2 was poised to move from an office-based business to a virtual model, we went through the presentation and delivery stages. I immediately saw three group responses. The first were my champions. They loved the idea. The second group was in the middle, and were going to do whatever the company ended up asking them to do. The last group was afraid. They did not understand how this would work, or how it might affect their performance, job security and the company's stability.

Over the next few days, I noticed the champions having deep conversations with people in the other two groups. I pulled a few of the champions aside and asked what they were hearing – not to name names, but to gauge the overall responses. They related fears, theories and all sorts of wild conjecture I never expected to hear. This allowed me to adjust my message to meet the needs that they were expressing. Their fears were demons representing the unknown. So, we set up additional meetings to do two things.

First, we addressed concerns where we could and dispelled any misinformation that was being repeated. Second, I asked the champions to tell us what they were excited about. Little by little, as they spread the word through the entire company about all of the positive things they anticipated from the change, the afraid group dwindled. In fact, one of them later became a champion. The majority of the rest ended up in the middle group, willing to proceed and see what would happen. A few stragglers remained. I had the choice of ending our working relationship or converting them.

Guess what: everyone stayed. Here's how you can achieve a similar degree of accord, the very essence of company unity.

Winning over complicated people

Having great company culture does not guarantee that everyone will get along. We all have had to deal with tricky people in our working lives. Sometimes a recalcitrant person is embedded in the company, and their usefulness outweighs their personality flaws. Or, you and that person just may not click. In both scenarios, communication – and even this negotiation in adopting and supporting your initiative for change – is an opportunity for improvement. Trying to ignore or work around people who challenge us, drag their feet and fear change will rarely work. If you can create better understanding and get this person to join you in moving forward, though, your efforts will gain massive acceleration.

You don't have to be their buddy. But understanding their concerns as best you can and helping them move past the negativity is not only noble, but necessary to your forward trajectory. So sit down, one on one, and employ the positive techniques of appreciative inquiry that we discussed in Chapter 4. The first two 'Ds' of that methodology, discovery and dream, are ideally situated to an intimate chat. Discover what is working well for your employee now and dream about how that might improve as each pillar is put in place. Would it help to get immediate feedback from accounts via online surveys? Are there things that are compromising efficiency that they think management should know about?

In dealing with a less cooperative individual, here are some strategies to consider:

Be careful where you sit I introduced Mark Goulston and his book *Just Listen* in Chapter 8. In that book, Goulston wrote about the importance of where we sit when we want to ensure everyone is heard. He suggests levelling the playing field by sitting side by side. When we sit next to someone, we establish a more cooperative environment. When we sit across from someone, especially in difficult situations, our body language is perceived as more combative.

Start small Find common ground and make agreements on the easy things first. Suppose your employee is a lone wolf and is not looking forward to instituting team-based project management. Ask them to recall a collaboration that went well in the past. This will get them grounded and feeling safe as you move into larger objections.

Negotiate a fair exchange Be prepared to listen, before they will listen. That means making eye contact, asking open-ended questions, taking notes and hearing people out – even if they are angry. This is an excellent time to let them release their frustrations. But insist on a civil discourse. When they finish, ask them for the same courtesy. If they interrupt and attempt to take the conversation to darker places, remind them that you listened quietly and allowed them to speak and to be heard. Remind them as many times as it takes. Interrupting and dominating the speaking time is one subconscious strategy to avoid actually considering a change in their thoughts or preconceptions.

When in doubt, apologize Disarm them before they can counterattack. It doesn't matter if you think you did anything wrong; this is about being effective, not right. A simple 'I am sorry' is a great way to disarm someone who is upset or worried.

Use their name The best word in any language is your name. You can make a great first impression with anyone if you find a way to say their name several times in the first moments after meeting. This is a proven networking and selling strategy, and you are definitely doing both of those things in this situation. But here, you know the person. Using their name can also help you draw out their real feelings, and bring trust and calmness to the encounter. For example: 'Charles, how do you really feel?' or 'In a perfect world, how can Bonnie be happy with this?' Sometimes when people fly off the handle or say something ridiculous, I avoid reacting and instead say their name slowly. They often shrug and say, 'Okay, I didn't really mean that.'

Ask them to say it differently People don't always say what they mean, or express themselves fully the first time. If you are having communication breakdown, you can meet each other half-way. Avoid getting stuck in a repetitive cycle that only entrenches a negative outlook. If what they are saying does not make sense or is an obvious deterrent to progress, ask them: 'Can you put that differently?' Or, 'Can you say that another way?' Give them space to try again. Their second attempt is often more articulate and accurate and it gives them the option for a change of heart.

Enlist an envoy Some people with fixed mindsets might see acquiescence as losing a personal duel with you. If you reach that point, see if a colleague is willing to try. Another person will have a different relationship with your slow adopter, or a communication style that is better suited to the situation. If all else fails, one of your champions may be able to make a breakthrough.

Move towards group achievement

Up to this point, I have suggested how to work with stakeholders and expose employees to your concept and vision for change. If you have made those introductions and found acceptance, each team member is focused on the future – on making your company not only a good place to work, but a great one. Your journey to success has begun. But, journeys rarely take place in a straight line.

When culture improves, some people may take the exit. This is usually a good thing. Your company philosophy and goals have been refined, and they may no longer apply to every member. This might be a good time to revisit your company's mission, values, vision and customer service statements, and revise them, if necessary. You are going to need them.

The momentum generated by the process of cultural change will be enough to keep most of your group moving forward. But your staff roster will also change and grow, and new people will need to be guided into the flow. This means you will be talking about what culture is and is not far into the future. When you hit switchbacks and rough spots in the road, return to the tools and materials offered in this book.

Part 1's 'Foundations' and 'Evaluation' chapters will remind you of the definitions you need to share, and the driving motivations you need to harness, in order to win new converts to the culture cause. You can point to examples of great company culture, such as Southwest Airlines and Google, and mention what your company shares with them, like a belief in employee judgement and promotion of innovation. You can mention ways in which your company allows those who work there chances for autonomy, mastery and purpose. You can indicate by how you treat people that you appreciate diverse thinking styles and what they do for business.

Like construction in any big city, the building of culture never stops. As you raise and maintain each pillar, you must keep the cultural conversation alive. Never let the topic fall into the realm of assumption – keep on talking about it. Part 2 gave you seven levels to build on, and seven different conversations to have. As you witness the transformation, you will talk about how effective transparent communication and positive approaches to challenges are. As you measure performance to assess your progress, you will acknowledge the people whose efforts help the company move forward. In navigating market difficulties and new opportunities, your team will find unique company features to exploit. Everyone from management to part-time employees will listen well and be heard, and when mistakes are made, your team will use them as stepping stones to new and better ideas.

This may sound utopian, but it is really just a way to get the most out of all the little things that make up day-to-day work at your company. By pulling together, it becomes easier for each person, and the sum of accomplishments will be much greater than the parts. It is here that exponential business success is possible. Perhaps it is in helping individuals rise above all of the mundane tasks and personal foibles that a shared culture elevates a company's potential as a whole.

If that is the goal, Part 3 of this book is the final stretch of pavement that will get you there. In the previous chapter, I showed you how to turn the many corners between your cultural vision and practice. You used hard data and soft skills to persuade the powers that be to follow you along that course. In this chapter, you learned to overcome the remaining individual roadblocks to embracing this change. Hopefully, I have helped you find champions and persuade even the most reluctant of staff that great culture is the vehicle to great success.

You're off and running. Using the best-performing companies in the marketplace today as your 'mentors', you will emulate and, eventually, achieve the type of cultural environment that boosted them to the top tier. The only advice that remains for me to give you now is: persist.

Note

1 Kahneman, D (2010) [accessed 28 July 2017] The riddle of experience vs memory [Online] https://www.ted.com/talks/daniel_kahneman_the_riddle_of_experience_vs_memory

INDEX

Italics indicate a figure.

CPSIA information can be obtained
at www.ICGtesting.com
Printed in the USA
LVOW05s1600270218
568055LV00024B/381/P